Sleeves

DISCARDE

skills institute
press

Distributed By
Fox Chapel Publishing

FOX CHAPEL
PUBLISHING

A DIRECTORY OF DESIGN DETAILS AND TECHNIQUES

© 2011 by Skills Institute Press LLC
"Select-n-Stitch Fashion Elements" series trademark of Skills Institute Press
Published and distributed in North America by Fox Chapel Publishing Company, Inc.,
East Petersburg, PA.

Select-n-Stitch Fashion Elements: Sleeves is an original work, first published in 2011.

Portions of text and art previously published by and reproduced under license with Direct Holdings Americas Inc.

ISBN 978-1-56523-571-7

Library of Congress Cataloging-in-Publication Data

Sleeves.
     p. cm. -- (Select-n-stitch fashion elements)
  Includes index.
  ISBN 978-1-56523-571-7
  1. Sleeves. I. Fox Chapel Publishing.
  TT603.S57 2011
  646.2--dc22
                        2010047597

To learn more about the other great books from Fox Chapel Publishing,
or to find a retailer near you, call toll-free 800-457-9112 or visit us at
www.FoxChapelPublishing.com.

Note to Authors: We are always looking for talented authors to write new books.
Please send a brief letter describing your idea to
Acquisition Editor, 1970 Broad Street, East Petersburg, PA 17520.

Printed in China
First printing: June 2011

Table of Contents

Sleeves

Whether you're sewing a simple shirt or an elaborate gown, having the right instructions can make a difference in the success of a garment. With step-by-step illustrations and thorough instructions, Select-n-Stitch gives you the in-depth information you need to learn or refine a technique and sew garments successfully the first time.

Use the contents page and Select-n-Stitch guides to find common fashion elements, such as tailored shirt sleeves or cap sleeves, and then flip to the detailed instructions to learn the best methods for constructing them. Whether you're using commercial patterns, modifying patterns, or mixing and matching to make your own creation, use these instructions to complete your sewing projects beautifully.

Select-n-Stitch Sleeves, page 6

Sleeves are one of the fundamental elements of shirts, dresses, and jackets. Learn the best methods to attach common sleeve designs so they're balanced, straight, and attractive.

Restyling, page 84

If you have a shirt you like, but the sleeves aren't quite right, change them! Use these easy approaches to modify sleeves to suit your style.

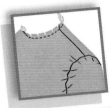

Fitting Set-In Sleeves,

Take the time to fit a pattern once, and then make stylish and appealing garments every time you sew. Learn how to adjust commercial patterns so they fit your body.

Buttons & Buttonholes,

Buttons are like jewelry for sleeves. Learn how to choose, place, size, and sew buttons, and sew strong, attractive buttonholes.

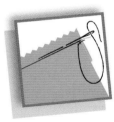

Basic Stitches & Techniques,

Not sure what an overcast stitch looks like or how to make a bias strip? Find straightforward instructions for key stitches and procedures.

Select-n-Stitch Sleeves

Sleeves are one of the fundamental elements of shirts, dresses, and jackets. Learn the best methods to attach common sleeve designs so they're balanced, straight, and attractive.

Cuffed Sleeves with Flat-Felled Seams, page 10

Set-In Sleeves with Hemmed Edges, page 24

Set-In Sleeves with Cuffs,

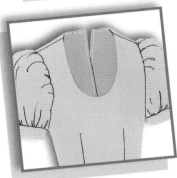

Short Puffed Sleeves,

One-Piece Raglan Sleeves,

Two-Piece Raglan Sleeves,

Dolman Sleeves, page 60

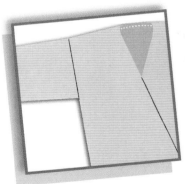

T-Shaped Kimono Sleeves, page 64

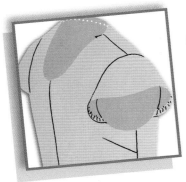

Cap Sleeves, page 68

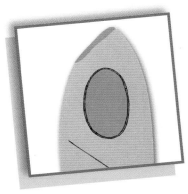

Bias-Faced Sleeveless Armholes, page 78

Cuffed Sleeves with Flat-Felled Seams

Preparing the cuff opening

1. To reinforce the area around the cuff opening, called the placket, machine stitch *(blue)*—without backstitching—from the bottom right edge of the pattern marking for the placket to the placket point, using 15 stitches per inch.

2. Raise the presser foot on your machine, turn the sleeve slightly, lower the presser foot and take one stitch across the placket point. Then raise the presser foot again, turn farther, lower the presser foot and continue stitching down the other side of the placket.

3. Cut a straight line up the middle of the V formed by the stitching, cutting to the placket point.

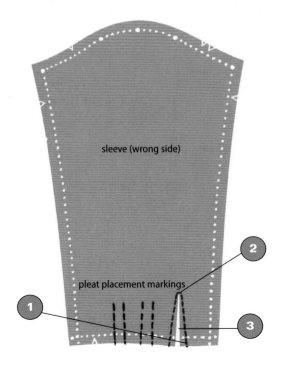

sleeve (wrong side)

pleat placement markings

Attaching the strip of fabric to the placket

4. From fabric leftover after you cut out the pattern, cut a strip along the lengthwise grain 1½ inches wide and twice the length of the closed placket.

5. Lay the strip wrong side down, spread open the placket, and place it wrong side down over the strip, aligning the ends of the placket with the outer corners of the strip.

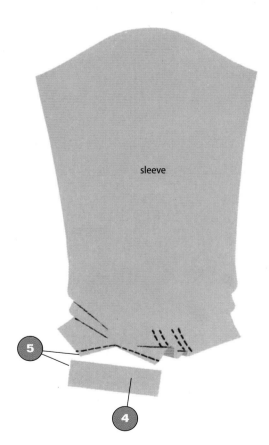

sleeve

Cuffed Sleeves with Flat-Felled Seams
Attaching the strip of fabric to the placket

6. Pin the strip to the placket, with the point of the placket ¼ inch in from the outer edge of the strip.

7. Baste (*red*) the strip to the placket, and remove the pins.

8. Machine stitch—resetting the machine to the normal 12 stitches per inch—in a straight line along the placket just inside the reinforcement stitches made in Step 1, pausing at the placket point to move the bunched-up fabric out of the way. Remove the basting.

9. Pull the unstitched edge of the strip from under the placket so that the strip projects wrong side up.

10. Press the seam allowance over the projecting strip.

11. Fold in the outer edge of the strip ¼ inch and press.

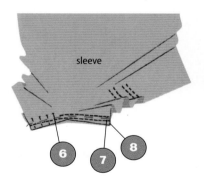

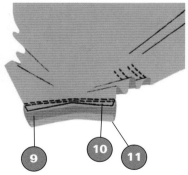

Enclosing the placket

12. Pin the folded outer edge of the strip to the placket so that it just covers the lines of machine stitching.

13. Baste and remove the pins.

14. Machine stitch along the folded edge, spreading the placket farther open as you go; pause at the point of the placket to redistribute the bunched-up fabric. Remove the basting and press.

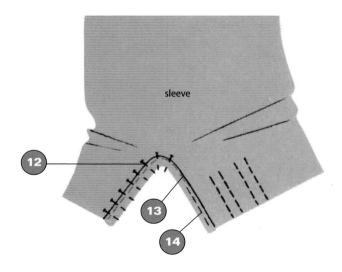

sleeve

Cuffed Sleeves with Flat-Felled Seams
Enclosing the placket

15. Turn the sleeve over so that it is wrong side up.

16. Fold one side under along the placket line. Without backstitching, machine stitch on a diagonal from the point of the placket to a spot ¼ inch down on its outer edge.

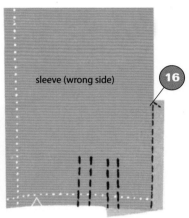

sleeve (wrong side)

16

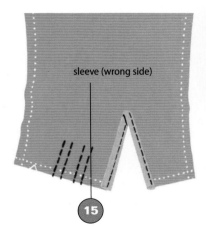

sleeve (wrong side)

15

Pleating the bottom of the sleeve

17. To make pleats at the places indicated on the pattern, turn the sleeve right side up, to the side that will be visible in the finished garment, and open it out flat.

18. Fold the pleats along their markings *(green)* toward the placket, then pin them.

19. Turn under the front lap of the placket—that is, the side closest to the pleats—and hold it and the pleats in place by basting along the bottom stitching line. Remove the pins.

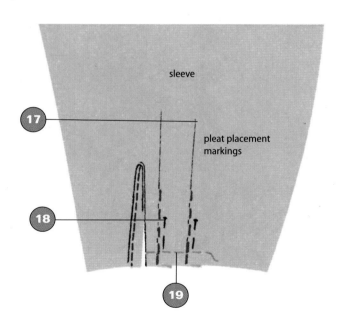

sleeve

pleat placement markings

Cuffed Sleeves with Flat-Felled Seams
Easing the sleeve

20. Turn the sleeve wrong side out. Machine baste—six stitches per inch—between the pattern markings *(white)* that indicate where extra fabric will be eased, making two parallel lines of basting ¼ inch apart along the top of the sleeve.

21. Pull the loose threads gently, first at one end, then at the other, to distribute the easing evenly.

22. Pin the sleeve to the armhole of the shirt body, all sections wrong sides out, matching dots, notches and seam intersections.

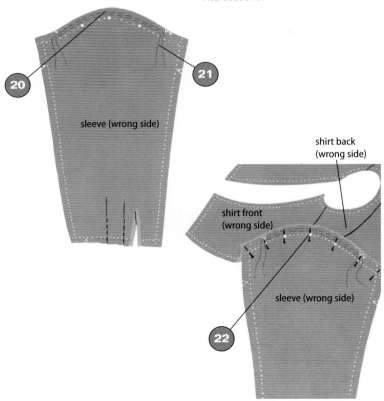

sleeve (wrong side)

shirt back
(wrong side)

shirt front
(wrong side)

sleeve (wrong side)

Stitching the sleeve to the body section

23. Distribute the eased fabric evenly until the sleeve fits smoothly into the armhole. Add pins as necessary.

24. Baste the sleeve to the body section, remove the pins, then machine stitch. Remove the basting, but leave in the ease lines.

25. Press both seam allowances toward the body section. Turn the garment right side out and press again.

26. Turn the garment wrong side out and construct a flat-felled seam *(pages 148–149)* around the armhole.

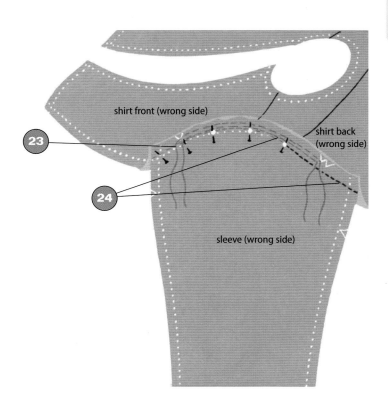

shirt front (wrong side)

23

shirt back (wrong side)

24

sleeve (wrong side)

Cuffed Sleeves with Flat-Felled Seams
Making the side seam

27. With the wrong sides of the fabric facing out, bring the side and underarm seams together, and pin the front of the body section to the back at the intersection of the armhole seam.

28. Pin the underarm seam of the sleeve, then pin the side seam of the body section, matching the notches.

29. Baste along the underarm seam and the side seam in one continuous line. Remove the pins.

30. Machine stitch from the bottom of the sleeve to the shirttail in one continuous line. Remove the basting.

31. Press both seam allowances toward the back of the garment and construct a continuous flat-felled seam *(pages 148–149)* along the sleeve and body section.

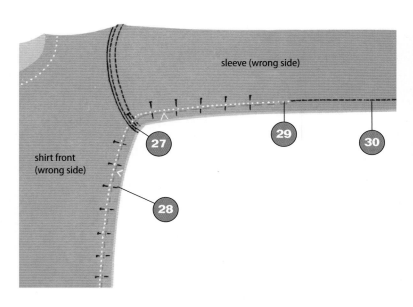

sleeve (wrong side)

shirt front
(wrong side)

Attaching the interfacing and facing to the cuff

32. Lay the cuff down wrong side up. Place the interfacing *(dark gray)* on top and pin together.

33. Baste just outside the stitching line. Remove the pins.

34. Trim away the interfacing all around the basting.

35. Fold in the top edge of the cuff along the stitching line and press.

36. Trim the folded edge to ¼ inch.

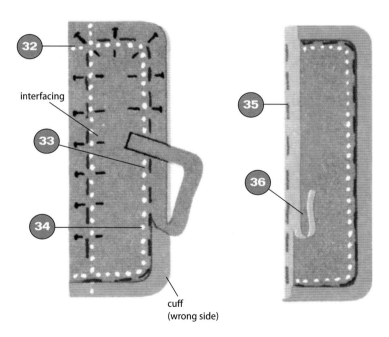

interfacing

cuff
(wrong side)

Cuffed Sleeves with Flat-Felled Seams
Attaching the interfacing and facing to the cuff

37. Place the cuff facing wrong side down and cover with the interfaced cuff wrong side up. Pin together.

38. Baste along the three outer sides, leaving the folded edge open. Remove the pins.

39. Machine stitch along the three basted sides.

40. Trim the seam allowance to ¼ inch around the three stitched sides; the facing will extend on the fourth side of the cuff. Remove the basting.

41. If the cuff is rounded, clip into the corners.

42. Turn the cuff right side out and press it and its extended facing flat.

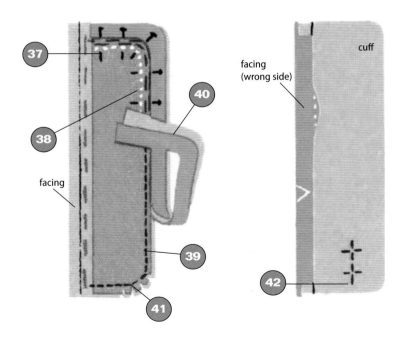

facing

facing

cuff

facing (wrong side)

Attaching the cuff to the sleeve

43. Turn the sleeve right side out and curl up the bottom edge.

44. Holding the cuff so that the wrong side of the facing is toward you, pin the extension of the cuff facing to the curled-up bottom of the sleeve. Match notches.

45. Hand baste the cuff facing to the sleeve, then remove the pins.

46. Machine stitch the facing to the sleeve, following the stitching line. Remove the basting.

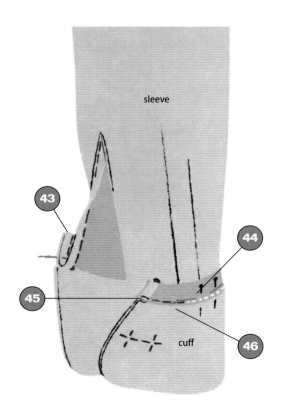

sleeve

cuff

Cuffed Sleeves with Flat-Felled Seams
Completing the cuff

47. Slip the bottom seam allowances between the cuff facing and interfacing. Press, then trim to ¼ inch.

48. Pin the folded edge of the cuff just over the stitching line of the sleeve.

49. Hand baste, then remove the pins.

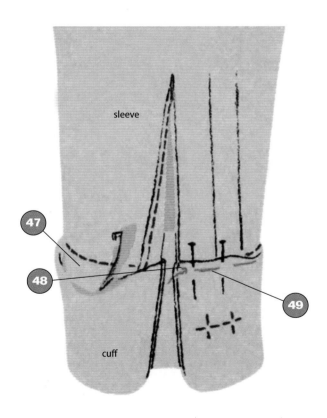

sleeve

cuff

50. Machine stitch along the folded edge, sewing at the top of the cuff from one edge of the placket to the other. Then pivot the cuff in the machine and stitch all along the outer edge of the cuff. When you reach the top edge of the cuff again, secure the last stitches by backstitching. Remove the basting.

51. Machine stitch a second line all around the cuff ¼ inch in from the stitching line made in Step 50.

52. Following the basted pattern markings for buttonhole positions, make buttonholes and attach buttons (pages 134–139).

53. Repeat the preceding steps on the other sleeve.

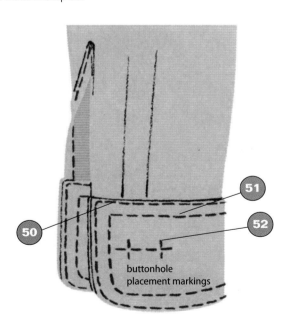

buttonhole placement markings

Set-in Sleeves with Hemmed Edges
Preparing the sleeve

1. To mark the center line of the sleeve, spread the sleeve open, wrong side up, and measure halfway in from the underarm seam lines at the hemline; then, draw a chalk line connecting this point to the pattern marking indicating the center of the sleeve cap. Run a line of basting stitches along the chalk-marked center line.

2. Run a line of basting stitches horizontally across the sleeve, joining the two points where the markings for the underarm seams meet the markings for the seam along the top curved edge of the sleeve.

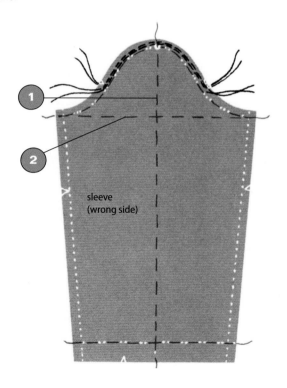

sleeve
(wrong side)

3. Run a line of basting along the hemline at the bottom of the sleeve, if one is indicated on your pattern.

4. Run a line of basting stitches along the seam line around the top curved edge of the sleeve, or cap.

5. Make two parallel lines of machine basting—six stitches to the inch— along the cap of the sleeve between the pattern markings indicating where the sleeve will be eased into the armhole. One line of basting should be ⅛ inch outside the seam-line marking stitched in Step 4, the other ⅛ inch outside the first. Leave 4-inch-long loose threads at each end.

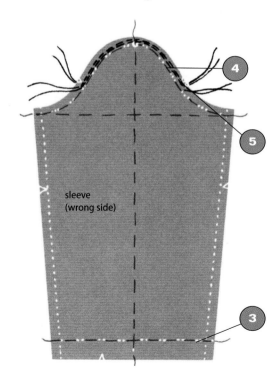

sleeve
(wrong side)

Set-in Sleeves with Hemmed Edges
Joining the underarm seam

6. Fold the sleeve in half, wrong side out, matching the intersection between the underarm seam and the cap seam, then matching the notches. Pin along the underarm seam at 1-to 2-inch intervals. Baste and remove the pins.

7. Machine stitch at the normal 12 stitches per inch along the underarm seam. Remove the bastings, and press the seam open.

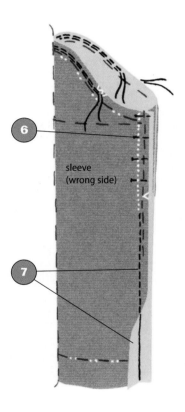

sleeve
(wrong side)

Easing the sleeve cap

8. Turn the sleeve right side out and press the underarm seam again, using a press cloth.

9. With the sleeve right side out, gently pull the loose threads of the basting stitches made in Step 5—first from one end, then from the other—to adjust the fullness of the sleeve cap, "easing" it to fit the armhole. As this action gathers the fabric, push it into small, even ripples on each side of the lengthwise basting made in Step 1. Continue easing, working the fabric and the threads until the sleeve cap is approximately the size of the armhole of the body section.

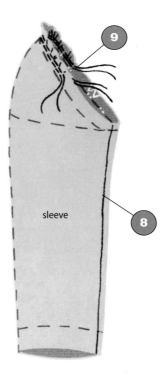

sleeve

Set-in Sleeves with Hemmed Edges
Aligning the sleeve

10. Test the alignment of the sleeve by holding it up with the crossed bastings made in Steps 1 and 2 facing you. The lengthwise bastings must hang exactly vertical and the crosswise bastings must cross the lengthwise ones at a precise right angle. If either line is askew, redistribute the easing of the sleeve cap made in Step 9.

11. Smooth away all the ripples in the eased cap ½ inch on each side of the lengthwise basting.

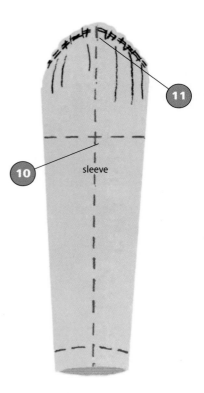

sleeve

Attaching the sleeve

12. Turn the assembled body section of the garment wrong side out. If you have not already done so, baste a row of stitches around the pattern markings for the armhole seam line.

13. Slip the sleeve into the armhole of the body section, and align the lengthwise bastings of the sleeve with the shoulder seam of the garment.

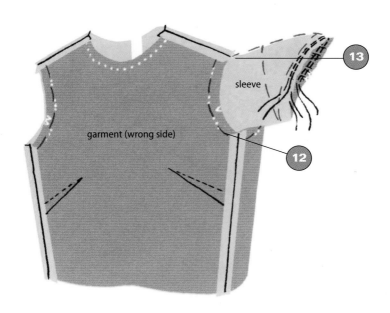

sleeve

garment (wrong side)

Set-in Sleeves with Hemmed Edges
Attaching the sleeve

14. Roll the sleeve cap over the armhole of the body section. Align the center marking on the garment shoulder seam with the lengthwise sleeve bastings at the cap end of the sleeve; insert a pin at the seam line. Match the underarm seam of the sleeve to the body section side seam and pin there. Then match and pin the notches.

15. Starting at the top of the sleeve cap, pin around the armhole in both directions, matching seam lines and placing pins at ¾-inch intervals.

16. Hand baste the sleeve to the armhole, sewing along the seam line. Remove the pins.

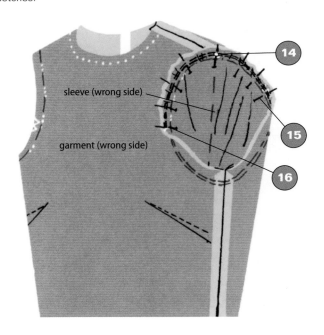

sleeve (wrong side)

garment (wrong side)

Trying on the garment

17. Turn the garment right side out and try it on to be sure the basted-in sleeve fits perfectly at the armhole; the basted alignment lines made in Steps 1 and 2 must be perpendicular and parallel to the floor and the ease gathering at the armhole should be evenly distributed. If either line is askew, re-set the sleeve.

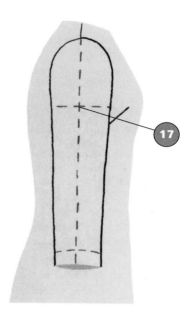

Set-in Sleeves with Hemmed Edges
Stitching the sleeve to the body section

18. Turn the body section wrong side out. Tuck the sleeve into the armhole.

19. Partially smooth the easing, or fullness, of the sleeve cap seam allowance by pressing it lightly with the tip of the iron. Do not press beyond the seam line.

20. Starting at the underarm seam, machine stitch the sleeve to the garment all around the armhole, sewing on the side of the bastings away from the seam allowance.

21. Reinforce the underarm seam of the sleeve with a second row of machine stitches between the notches, stitching into the seam allowance ¼ inch away from the machine stitching made in Step 20. Remove all bastings.

22. Clip into the underarm seam allowance at the notches. Cut up to but not through the reinforcement stitches made in Step 21, then trim along the machine stitching. Taper the ends so that the rest of the seam allowance is trimmed to ½ inch.

23. Press the underarm seam allowance over the reinforcement stitches. With the tip of the iron, press the remaining seam allowance as in Step 19.

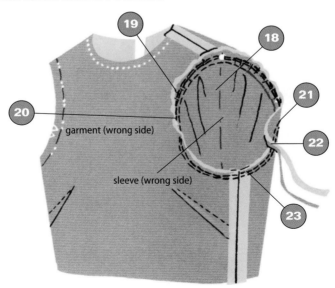

garment (wrong side)

sleeve (wrong side)

Finishing the sleeve hem

24. Pull the sleeve out through the armhole so that it is wrong side out, and enclose the raw edge at the bottom of the sleeve with a Hong Kong hem *(pages 150–153)*.

25. Turn the hem up along the basting line made in Step 3, and pin. Hand baste close to the fold. Remove the pins.

26. Pin and baste the finished edge to the sleeve. Remove the pins.

27. Handstitch the hem to the sleeve with a blind hemming stitch *(page 140)*. Remove all bastings and press on the wrong side.

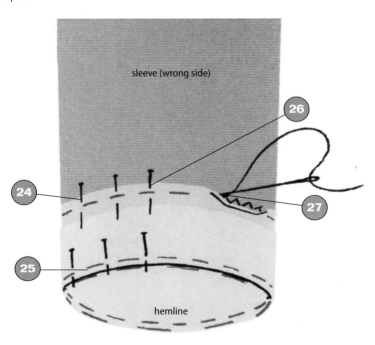

sleeve (wrong side)

hemline

Set-in Sleeves with Cuffs

Preparing the cuff opening

1. Prepare the cuff and sleeve placket per the instructions for Cuffed Sleeves with Flat-Felled Seams, Steps 1–16 (*pages 10–14*).

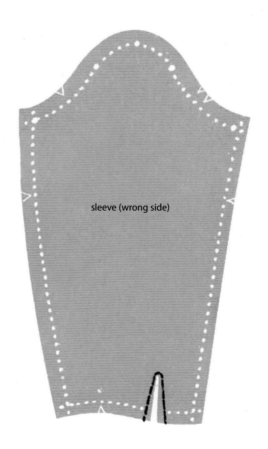

sleeve (wrong side)

Making the sleeve seam

2. Open the sleeve out flat, wrong side up, and machine baste—six stitches per inch—between the pattern markings *(white)* used to indicate the area where extra fabric will be eased, making two parallel lines ¼ inch apart along the top of the sleeve.

3. Fold the sleeve in half, wrong sides out, and pin along the underarm seam, matching and pinning first at the seam intersection, next at the notches, then at any other pattern markings. Add more pins at 1- to 2-inch intervals.

4. Baste from the armhole to the end of the sleeve, then remove the pins.

5. Machine stitch—resetting the machine to the normal 12 stitches per inch–from the armhole to the end of the sleeve, then remove the basting.

6. Press the seam open on a sleeve board.

7a. If the sleeve edge is gathered, make two parallel ease lines ¼ inch apart, as in Step 2, in the seam allowance at the bottom of the sleeve, starting and ending ½ inch from the placket.

7b. If the sleeve edge is pleated, follow the instructions for Cuffed Sleeves with Flat-Felled seams, Step 17.

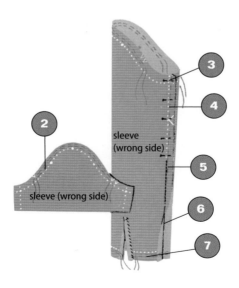

sleeve (wrong side)

sleeve (wrong side)

Set-in Sleeves with Cuffs
Attaching the interfacing to the cuff

8. Lay the cuff down, wrong side up. Place the interfacing *(dark gray)* on top and pin the two together on the three outer sides, matching notches or other pattern markings. Leave the inside edge open.

9. Baste the three outer sides just outside the stitching line. Remove the pins, and trim the interfacing.

10. Attach the open edge of the interfacing to the cuff using a hemming stitch *(page 143)*.

11. On the half of the cuff that has no interfacing, fold in the outer edge along the stitching line. Press, and trim the folded edge to ¼ inch.

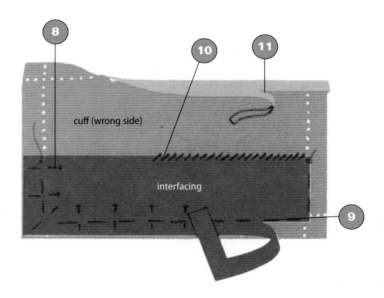

cuff (wrong side)

interfacing

Attaching the cuff to the sleeve

12. With the sleeve wrong side out, gently pull the loose ease threads sewn in Step 7a to begin adjusting the ease.

13. Turn up the bottom of the interfaced half of the cuff.

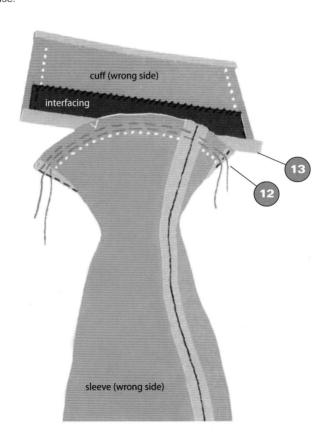

cuff (wrong side)

interfacing

sleeve (wrong side)

Set-in Sleeves with Cuffs
Attaching the cuff to the sleeve

14. Pin the sleeve to the cuff along its turned-up edge, matching notches.

15. Align the stitching lines of the cuff edges with the outer edges of the placket; if your pattern calls for the cuff to extend beyond the placket, disregard the cuff stitching lines on the extension and match notches and other pattern markings.

16. To ease the sleeve into the cuff, pull the loose ease threads, first at one end, then at the other, gradually distributing the easing until the sleeve fits the cuff. Secure with additional pins at ½-inch intervals.

17. Hand baste just below the ease lines. Remove the pins and machine stitch.

18. Trim the two layers of the seam allowance—sleeve and cuff—¼ inch from the stitching line. Remove the basting, then press the trimmed seam allowance toward the cuff.

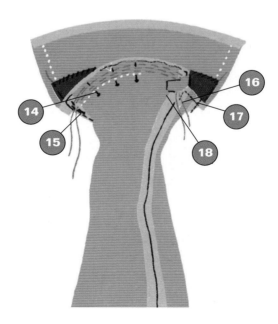

Stitching the ends of the cuff

19. Turn the sleeve right side out. Fold the cuff in half along its fold line so that it is wrong side out.

20. Pin the open ends of the cuff together and baste. Remove the pins.

21. Machine stitch the ends together, sewing a few stitches off the edge of the fabric. Tie off the threads.

22. Trim the seam allowances to ¼ inch and remove the basting.

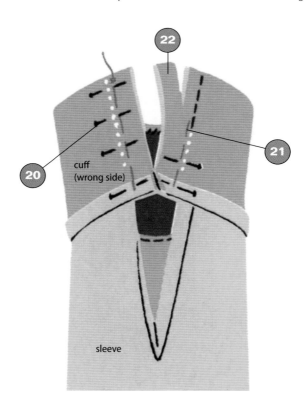

cuff
(wrong side)

sleeve

Set-in Sleeves with Cuffs
Completing the cuff

23. Turn the sleeve wrong side out. Turn the cuff right side out.

24. Pin the edge of the cuff over the stitching line of the sleeve and baste. Remove the pins.

25. Stitch the cuff to the sleeve with a hemming stitch *(page 143)* along the edge. Do not stitch into the fabric beneath the folded edge but pick up only the thread from the machine stitching made in Step 17. Remove the basting.

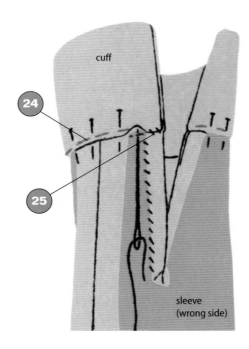

cuff

sleeve
(wrong side)

Inserting the sleeve into the armhole

26. Insert and stitch the sleeve following the instructions for Set-in Sleeves with Hemmed Edges, Steps 12–23 *(pages 29–32)*.

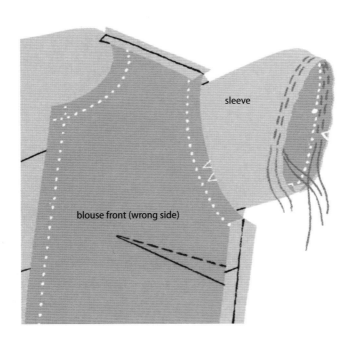

sleeve

blouse front (wrong side)

Short Puffed Sleeves
Preparing the sleeve

1. Make two parallel rows of machine basting (6 stitches to the inch) around the curved upper edge, or cap, of the sleeve between the pattern markings (usually notches) indicating where the fullness of the sleeve will be gathered. Sew one line of machine basting just outside the seam line, the other ¼ inch outside the first. Leave 4-inch-long loose threads at each end of the bastings.

2. Repeat Step 1 along the lower edge of the sleeve, between the pattern markings (usually small circles) indicating where the fullness will be gathered.

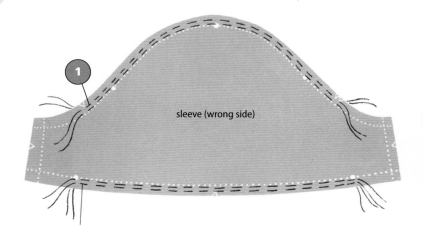

sleeve (wrong side)

Preparing the sleeve band

3. Place the sleeve band on a flat surface, wrong side up, with the notched edge at the top. Fold over the unnotched edge of the band along the seam-line marking and press.

4. Trim the folded edge to ¼ inch.

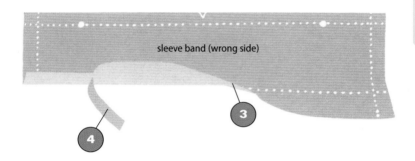

sleeve band (wrong side)

Short Puffed Sleeves
Attaching the sleeve band to the sleeve

5. Align the notched edge of the sleeve band with the lower edge of the sleeve.

6. Gently pull the loose threads of the machine basting made in Step 2; pull only the threads on the underside (which came from the machine's bobbin instead of the needle) because the fabric will slide over them more easily. Pull the basting threads first from one end, then from the other—gathering the fullness of the lower edge of the sleeve until it is approximately the same size as the sleeve band.

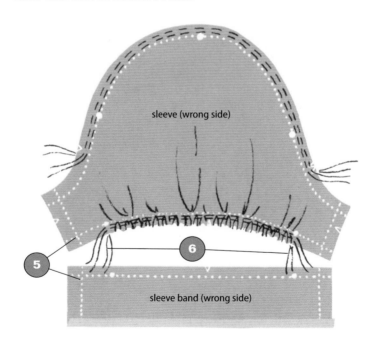

sleeve (wrong side)

sleeve band (wrong side)

7. Pin the sleeve band to the sleeve, matching the notches at the center and the seam-line markings at the outer edges.

8. Pull the ends of the loose threads of the machine basting again and continue to gather the fabric until the sleeve fits the band perfectly. Then add more pins at ½-inch intervals.

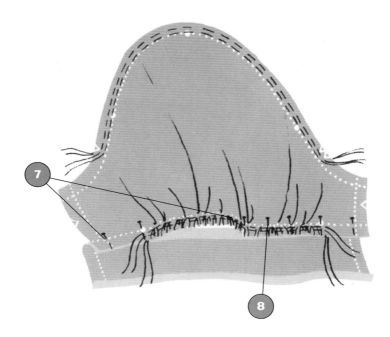

Short Puffed Sleeves
Stitching the sleeve band to the sleeve

9. Hand baste the sleeve band to the sleeve, sewing just outside the seam-line marking at the lower edge of the sleeve. As you baste, readjust the gathers, if necessary, so that they are evenly distributed. Remove the pins.

10. Reset the machine to the normal 12 stitches to the inch and stitch along the sleeve seam line. Remove the basting made in Step 9.

11. Trim the seam allowances of the sleeve and the sleeve band to ¼ inch.

12. Fold the trimmed seam allowances toward the sleeve band and press them lightly with the tip of the iron. Do not press beyond the line of machine stitching.

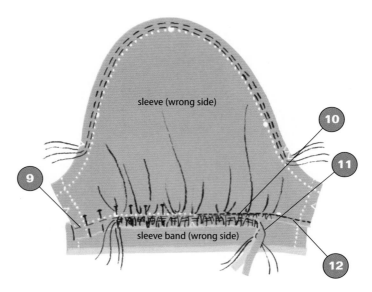

sleeve (wrong side)

sleeve band (wrong side)

Joining the underarm seam

13. Fold the sleeve in half, wrong side out, with the band extending away from the sleeve.

14. Pin the edges of the sleeve together along the underarm seam line, matching the pattern markings and making sure that both ends of the line of machine stitching that attaches the band to the sleeve are aligned as they meet at the underarm seam.

15. Baste just outside the seam line. Remove the pins.

16. Machine stitch along the seam line from the top of the underarm edge to the folded bottom edge of the band. Remove the bastings.

17. Press the seam open.

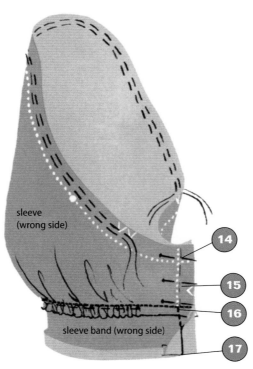

sleeve
(wrong side)

sleeve band (wrong side)

Short Puffed Sleeves
Finishing the sleeve band

18. Turn up the folded edge of the sleeve band so that it covers the line of machine stitching attaching the band to the sleeve.

19. Pin the band to the sleeve at ½-inch intervals.

20. Hand baste the band to the sleeve, sewing just below the folded edge of the band. Remove the pins.

21. Attach the edge of the band to the sleeve, using a slip stitch *(Appendix)*. Sew through the threads of the machine stitching rather than through the garment fabric, so that the stitches will not be visible on the outside of the sleeve.

22. Remove the bastings and press.

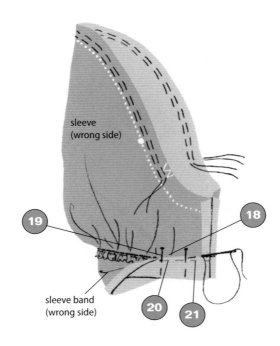

sleeve
(wrong side)

sleeve band
(wrong side)

Fitting the sleeve to the garment

23. If you have not already done so, assemble the garment bodice according to your pattern instructions and turn it wrong side out.

24. Turn the sleeve right side out and gently pull the loose bobbin threads of the basting made in Step 1: they are now on the outside of the garment.

Pull first from one end, then from the other—gathering the fullness of the sleeve cap until it is approximately the size of the garment armhole.

25. Slip the sleeve into the armhole, with the underarm sleeve seam facing the side seam of the garment.

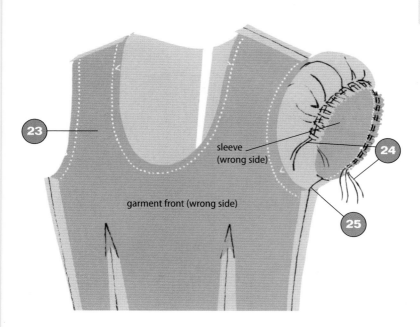

23

24

25

sleeve (wrong side)

garment front (wrong side)

Short Puffed Sleeves
Pinning the sleeve to the garment

26. Roll the top of the sleeve over the armhole of the garment and pin the sleeve to the garment, first matching the pattern marking indicating the top center of the sleeve—usually a large circle—to the shoulder seam of the garment.

27. Pin next at the point where the underarm seam of the sleeve meets the side seam of the garment. Then add pins to match notches and other pattern markings.

28. Pull the loose threads of the machine basting around the sleeve cap again and continue to gather the fabric until the sleeve cap fits the armhole.

29. Add more pins at ½-inch intervals around the sleeve, starting at the top center of the sleeve cap and working around the armhole in both directions.

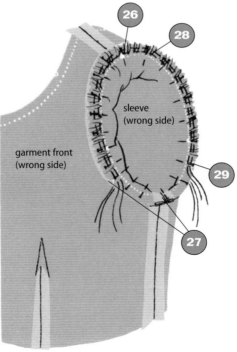

sleeve
(wrong side)

garment front
(wrong side)

Stitching the sleeve to the garment

30. Hand baste the sleeve to the garment just outside the sleeve seam line. As you baste, readjust the gathers, if necessary, so that they are evenly distributed. Remove the pins.

31. Machine stitch the sleeve to the garment along the sleeve seam line. Begin to stitch at the underarm seam and continue around the armhole. Remove the bastings.

32. Trim the seam allowances of the sleeve and the garment armhole to ¼ inch.

33. To prevent the fabric from raveling, sew the trimmed seam allowances together with an overcast stitch *(Appendix)* around the armhole.

34. Fold the seam allowances toward the sleeve and press them lightly with the tip of the iron. Do not press beyond the line of machine stitching.

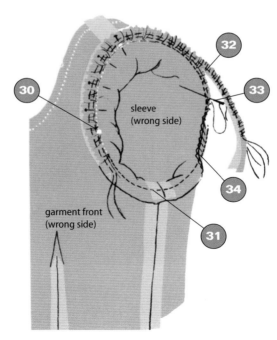

sleeve
(wrong side)

garment front
(wrong side)

One-Piece Raglan Sleeves
Making the sleeve underarm seam

1. Run a line of basting stitches along the seam-line markings around the armhole of the sleeve.

2. Run a line of basting along the hemline at the bottom of the sleeve, if one is indicated on your pattern.

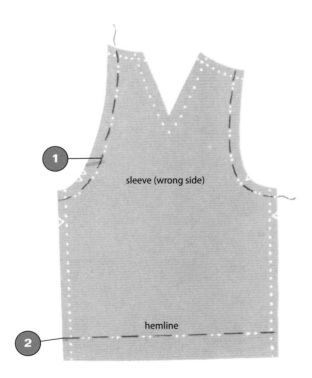

sleeve (wrong side)

hemline

3. Fold the sleeve in half, wrong side out, matching the points where the underarm and armhole seams intersect, and matching the notches on the underarm seam. Pin.

4. Baste the underarm seam outside the seam line, as close to it as possible. Remove the pins.

5. Machine stitch along the underarm seam line. Remove the bastings, and press the seam open.

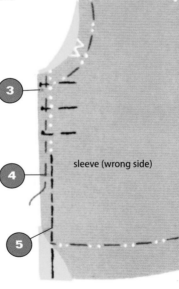

sleeve (wrong side)

One-Piece Raglan Sleeves
Attaching the sleeve to the body section

6. If you have not already done so, turn the assembled garment wrong side out and run a line of basting stitches around the armhole seam line.

7. Turn the sleeve right side out and slip it into the armhole of the body section. Place the sleeve and the body section together and pin, matching the notches, the basting stitches made in Steps 1 and 6, and the intersection between the sleeve underarm seam and the side seam of the body section.

8. Baste all around the armhole just outside the basted line marking the sleeve seam line. Remove the pins.

9. Machine stitch on the sleeve seam line all around the armhole. Start at the point where the top of the sleeve meets the garment back. Remove the bastings.

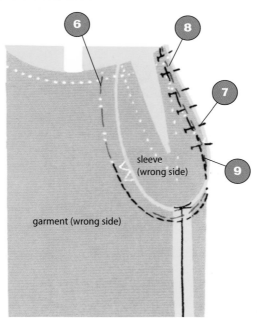

sleeve (wrong side)

garment (wrong side)

10. To reinforce the underarm area, make a second row of machine stitching between the notches, stitching ¼ inch into the seam allowance.

11. Clip into the underarm seam allowance at the notches up to, but not through, the reinforcement stitches and trim close to the stitches.

12. Press open the untrimmed seam allowances above the clipping, placing brown wrapping paper between the seam allowances and the garment fabric to prevent marks on the outside of the garment.

13. Press the trimmed seam allowance flat.

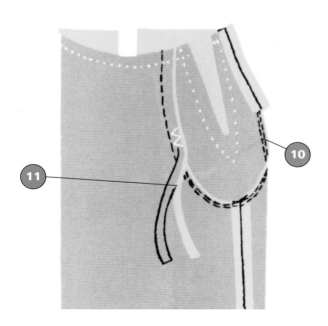

One-Piece Raglan Sleeves
Making the dart seam

14. Pin closed the dart seam—which, unlike the standard dart, is cut open at one end. Match the dart seam lines and the intersection between the dart seam and the neck seam line at the shoulder or upper edge of the sleeve. Baste the dart seam just outside the seam line. Remove the pins.

15. Machine stitch the dart seam, beginning at the neckline and sewing a few stitches off the point of the dart. Tie off the ends of the machine threads at the point. Remove the bastings.

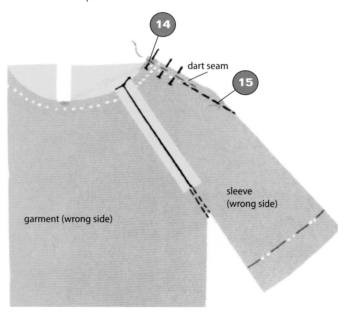

dart seam

sleeve
(wrong side)

garment (wrong side)

16. Press the dart seam open, placing brown wrapping paper between the seam allowances of the dart seam and the garment fabric to prevent marks that may show on the outside of the garment.

17. Finish the hem at the bottom of the sleeve as shown in the directions for Set-In Sleeves with Hemmed Edges, Steps 24–27 *(page 33)*.

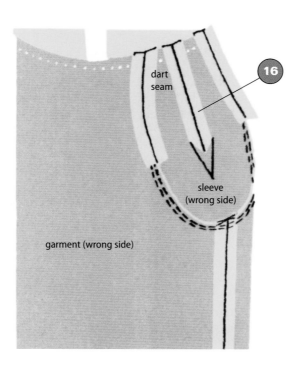

dart
seam

16

sleeve
(wrong side)

garment (wrong side)

Two-Piece Raglan Sleeves

Making the underarm and shoulder seams

1. Run a line of basting stitches along the seam-line markings around the armhole of the front and back sleeve sections.

2. Run a line of basting along the hemline at the bottom of the sleeve, if one is indicated on your pattern.

3. Pin the front and back sections of the sleeve together at the underarm seam. Match the seam intersections and notches.

4. Baste the underarm seam as closely as possible outside the seam line. Remove the pins.

5. Machine stitch along the underarm seam line. Remove the bastings and press the seam open.

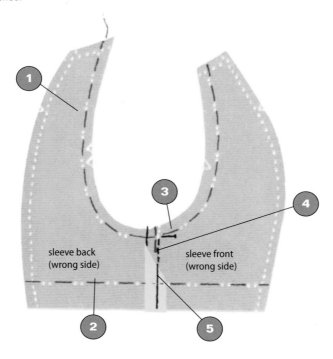

sleeve back
(wrong side)

sleeve front
(wrong side)

6. Attach the sleeve to the body section by following the instructions for One-Piece Raglan Sleeves, Steps 6–13 *(pages 54–55)*.

7. Finish the hem at the bottom of the sleeve as shown in the instructions for Set-in Sleeves with Hemmed Edges, Steps 24–27 *(page 33)*.

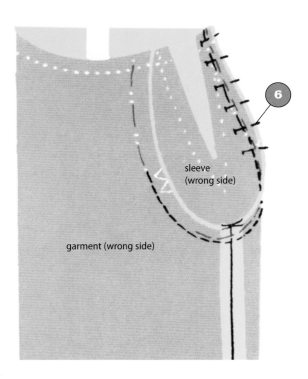

sleeve
(wrong side)

garment (wrong side)

Dolman Sleeves
Preparing the back of the sleeve

1. To join the left and right bodice back pieces (which include the sleeve backs), stitch the center back seam and press it open. (At this point the zipper or other closure should be finished.) Make sure any darts are stitched and pressed. Then turn the bodice back wrong side up.

2. To reinforce the underarm curve of the sleeve, start by machine stitching just outside the underarm seam line between the pattern markings indicating the underarm curve—usually circles.

3. Clip straight into the seam allowances along the underarm curve at ½-inch intervals, cutting up to but not into the stitching.

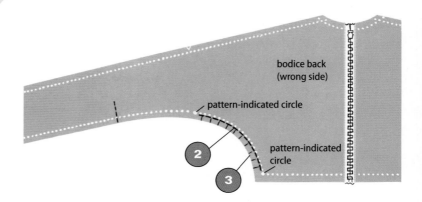

bodice back
(wrong side)

pattern-indicated circle

pattern-indicated circle

2

3

Preparing the front of the sleeve

4. To join the left and right bodice front pieces (which include the sleeve fronts), stitch the center front seam and press it open. Make sure any darts are stitched and pressed. Turn the bodice front wrong side up and reinforce as described in Steps 2 and 3.

5. To provide additional reinforcement of the underarm curve, start by measuring the distance between the pattern markings indicating the curve and cutting a length of seam tape to that measurement.

6. Center the tape over the seam line at one end of the underarm curve and fit the tape to the curve by pulling it straight so that the clips spread apart and pinning the tape to the curve at 1-inch intervals. Baste the tape to the seam allowance ⅛ inch from the edge of the tape. Remove the pins.

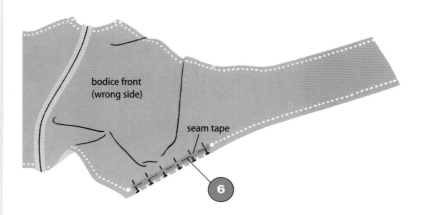

bodice front
(wrong side)

seam tape

6

Dolman Sleeves
Finishing the shoulder and top sleeve seam

7. Place the bodice back wrong side down and set the bodice front on top of it, wrong side up.

8. Matching the pattern markings, pin the front and back bodice pieces together at 2-inch intervals along the shoulder and top sleeve seam line, from the neckline edge to the end of the sleeve.

9. Baste the bodice pieces together just outside the shoulder and top sleeve seam line. Remove the pins.

10. Machine stitch along the seam line from the end of the sleeve to the neckline edge. Remove the basting.

11. Press the seam open.

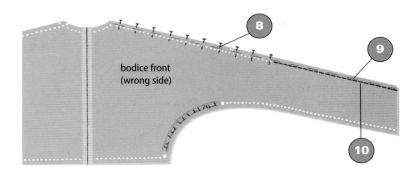

bodice front
(wrong side)

Finishing the side and underarm seams

12. Pin the front and back bodice pieces together at 2-inch intervals along the side and underarm seam line, matching the pattern markings.

13. Baste the bodice pieces together just outside the side and underarm seam line. (The basting on the underarm should run over the basting made on the seam tape in Step 6.) Remove the pins.

14. Machine stitch along the seam line and through the center of the tape from the end of the sleeve to the bottom of the bodice. Remove the bastings.

15. Turn the garment right side out.

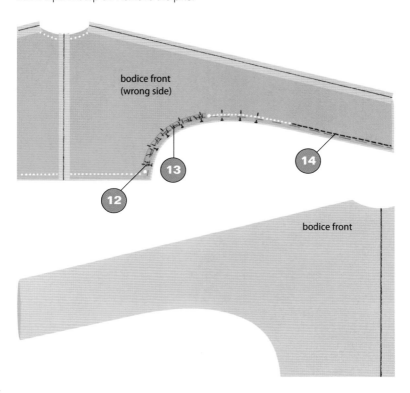

bodice front
(wrong side)

bodice front

T-Shaped Kimono Sleeves
Attaching the sleeve to the bodice

1. Stitch the bodice shoulder seams and press them open. Make sure any darts are stitched and pressed. Spread out the bodice, wrong side down.

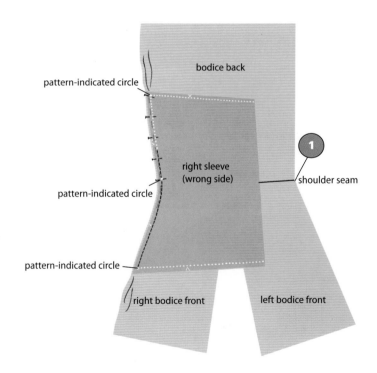

bodice back

pattern-indicated circle

right sleeve
(wrong side)

pattern-indicated circle

pattern-indicated circle

shoulder seam

right bodice front

left bodice front

2. Place the right sleeve wrong side up over the right half of the bodice, matching the notches and making sure that the pattern-indicated circle in the middle of the armhole seam line of the sleeve falls at the shoulder seam of the bodice and that the two end circles on the sleeve match the corresponding circles on the bodice.

3. Pin the sleeve to the bodice between the end circles along the edge of the armhole. Baste just outside the seam line. Remove the pins.

4. Machine stitch along the seam line, making sure not to stitch beyond the circles at the ends of the sleeve. Remove the basting.

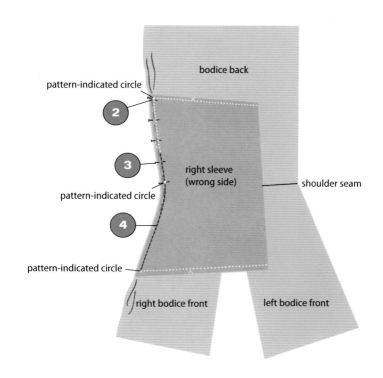

pattern-indicated circle

bodice back

right sleeve (wrong side)

shoulder seam

pattern-indicated circle

pattern-indicated circle

right bodice front

left bodice front

T-Shaped Kimono Sleeves
Stitching the side seam of the bodice

5. Turn the bodice wrong side out, and fold the bodice back under the bodice front.

6. Pin the bodice front and bodice back together at 2-inch intervals along the side seam line, matching the pattern markings.

7. Baste just outside the side seam line, keeping the underarm seam allowance of the sleeve out of the way. Remove the pins.

8. Machine stitch along the side seam line, starting just below the circle at the underarm of the sleeve. First go backward a few stitches to the circle to reinforce the seam. Then stitch to the bottom of the bodice. Remove the basting.

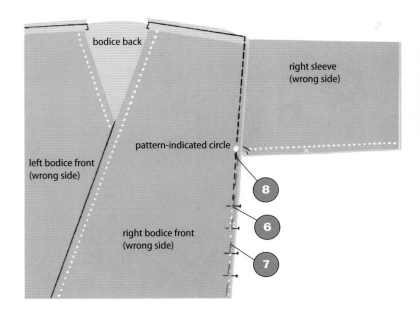

bodice back

right sleeve
(wrong side)

pattern-indicated circle

left bodice front
(wrong side)

right bodice front
(wrong side)

Stitching the underarm seam of the sleeve

9. Pin the underarm edges of the sleeve together at 2-inch intervals along the seam line, matching the pattern markings.

10. Baste just outside the underarm seam line, keeping the side seam allowance out of the way. Remove the pins.

11. Machine stitch along the underarm seam line, starting just beyond the circle. First go backward a few stitches to the circle to reinforce the seam. Then stitch to the outside edge of the sleeve. Remove the basting.

12. Press open the bodice side seam, the sleeve underarm seam and the armhole seam.

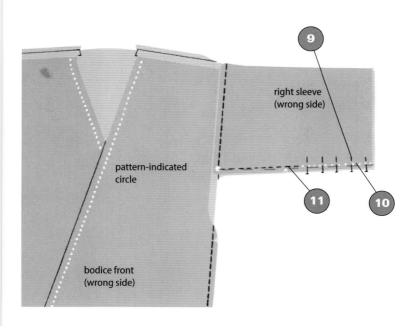

right sleeve
(wrong side)

pattern-indicated
circle

bodice front
(wrong side)

Cap Sleeves
Preparing the sleeve

1. Spread the sleeve wrong side out. Hem the unnotched edge.

2. On the armhole edge of the sleeve, run two parallel lines of machine basting (6 stitches to the inch) between the pattern markings—usually notches—indicating the area to be eased (*page 27*) into the bodice armhole. Make one basting line ⅛ inch outside the seam line and the other ¼ inch outside the first basting line. Leave 4 inches of loose thread at both ends of each line.

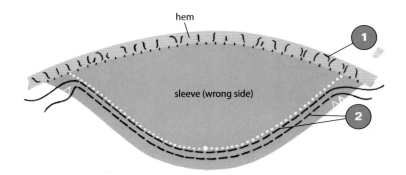

hem

sleeve (wrong side)

Pinning the sleeve to the armhole

3. Stitch the shoulder seams to join the front and back of the bodice. Press the seams open. Make sure any darts are stitched and pressed. Spread the bodice out wrong side down.

4. With the wrong side facing out, pin the sleeve to the bodice at the shoulder seam with the pattern-indicated circle on the sleeve matched exactly to the shoulder seam.

5. To ease the sleeve so it will fit the bodice armhole, pull the two basting threads on the front half of the sleeve until the notch on the front half of the sleeve matches the corresponding notch on the bodice front. Pin the sleeve to the bodice at the notches. Adjust the easing evenly.

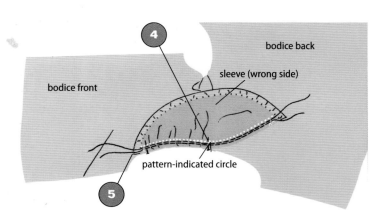

bodice back

sleeve (wrong side)

bodice front

pattern-indicated circle

Cap Sleeves
Pinning the sleeve to the armhole

6. Pin the sleeve to the bodice front at ½-inch intervals along the seam line, starting at the pattern-indicated circle.

7. Repeat Steps 5 and 6 on the back half of the sleeve and the bodice back.

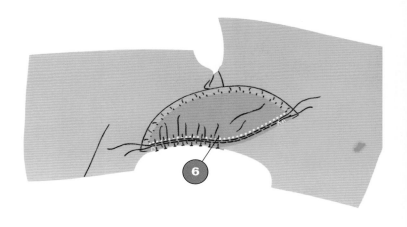

Attaching the sleeve to the armhole

8. Baste the sleeve just outside the seam line where it has been pinned to the bodice. Keep the gathers formed by the easing from extending into the basting. Remove the pins.

9. Machine stitch along the seam line, making sure the gathers remain below the stitching. Remove the bastings made in Step 8.

10. To reinforce the armhole seam made in Step 9, run a second line of machine stitching ¼ inch outside the first line.

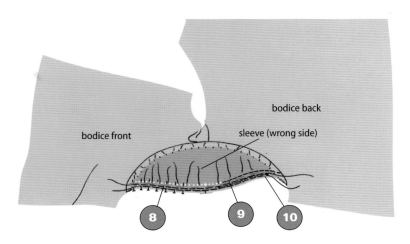

bodice back

bodice front

sleeve (wrong side)

Cap Sleeves
Attaching the sleeve to the armhole

11. Trim the seam allowance of the sleeve, cutting as close to the outer line of machine stitching as possible.

12. Trim the seam allowance of the bodice along the sleeve, leaving it ⅟₁₆ inch wider than the sleeve seam allowance.

13. Press the trimmed seam allowances toward the bodice.

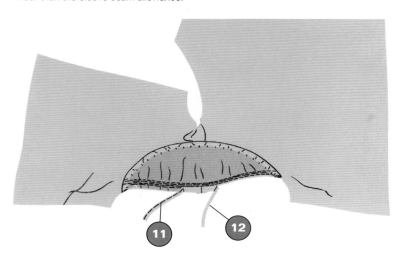

Stitching the side seams of the bodice

14. Pin the front and back bodice together at 2-inch intervals along the side seam line, wrong sides out. Baste just outside the seam line and remove the pins.

15. Try the garment on for fit.

16. Machine stitch and remove the bastings.

17. Press the seam open.

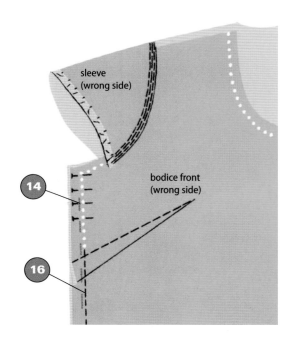

sleeve
(wrong side)

bodice front
(wrong side)

Cap Sleeves
Attaching tape to the underarm

18. Turn the garment right side out, and spread the armhole open.

19. Measure the seam line on the bottom part of the armhole that is formed only by the bodice.

20. Cut a piece of ½-inch-wide bias tape, 1 inch longer than the length measured in Step 19.

21. Unfold one side of the bias tape and pin it to the underarm curve, matching the fold line of the tape to the seam line and extending the tape ½ inch onto the lower edge of the sleeve hem at both ends.

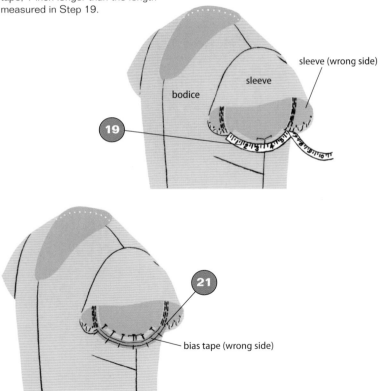

sleeve (wrong side)

sleeve

bodice

19

bias tape (wrong side)

21

22. Baste the bias tape to the underarm just above the fold line of the tape. Remove the pins.

23. Machine stitch along the fold line of the tape and remove the basting.

24. Trim the bodice underarm seam allowance to within 1/16 inch of the tape.

25. To keep the underarm seam allowance flat, clip straight into the tape and the bodice underarm seam allowance around the underarm at 1/2-inch intervals, cutting up to but not into the stitching.

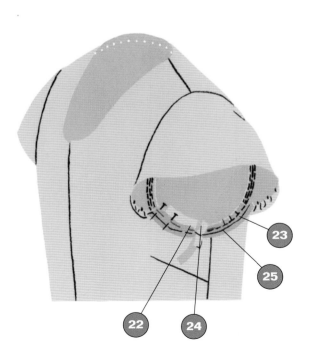

Cap Sleeves
Finishing the underarm

26. Turn the garment wrong side out and press the clipped tape and bodice seam allowance toward the bodice.

27. Fold the loose edge of the bias tape over the underarm seam to the wrong side of the bodice.

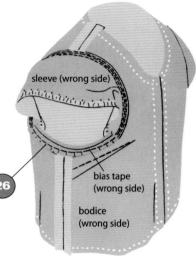

sleeve (wrong side)

bias tape
(wrong side)

bodice
(wrong side)

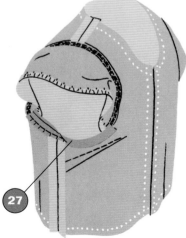

28. Roll the seam line just below the fold and pin the tape in place along the underarm curve at ½-inch intervals.

29. Attach the folded edge of the tape to the bodice, using a slip stitch *(page 145)*. Remove the pins.

30. Press the tape flat from the wrong side.

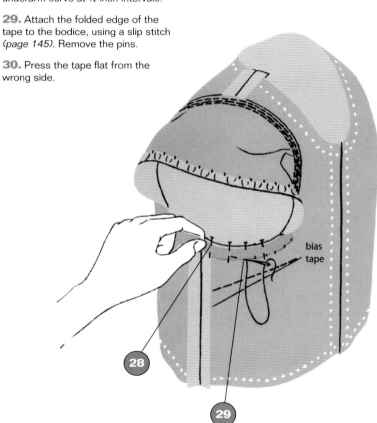

bias tape

Bias-Faced Sleeveless Armholes
Preparing the armhole

1. To prevent the fabric from stretching as you work, run a row of machine stitching just outside the armhole seam line of the assembled, underlined garment.

2. Trim the armhole seam allowance to ⅛ inch.

3. Remove the basting marking the armhole seam line.

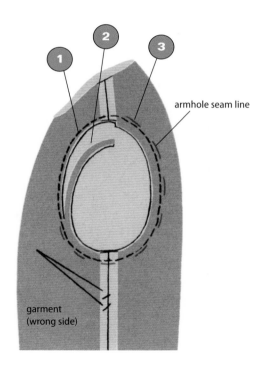

armhole seam line

garment
(wrong side)

Preparing the bias facing

4. Cut a bias strip *(pages 146–147)* 1⅜ inches wide and at least 3 inches longer than the armhole seam line. This strip is the armhole facing.

5. Cut the ends of the facing at right angles to the long edges.

6. Fold the facing in half, wrong sides together.

7. Using an iron, press the bias facing into a circular shape. Make sure the folded edge is on the outside.

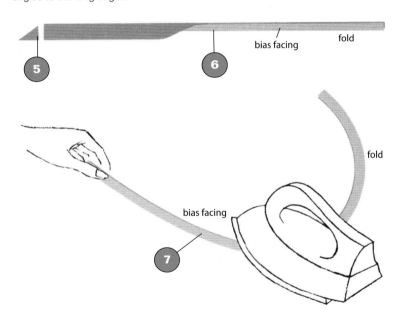

bias facing   fold

fold

bias facing

Bias-Faced Sleeveless Armholes
Attaching the facing to the armhole

8. With the garment turned right side out, arrange the armhole of the garment over the narrow end of an ironing board, as shown. Make sure the side seam is on top.

9. To pin the bias facing to the garment, start by turning up one end of the facing ¼ inch. Align the end with the side seam of the garment. Make sure the raw edges of the facing align with the raw edge of the armhole. Pin.

10. Using an iron to further shape the facing, continue to pin around the armhole. Rotate the garment around the ironing board as you work.

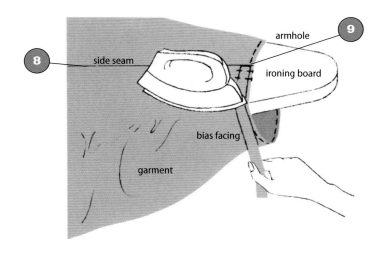

side seam

armhole

ironing board

bias facing

garment

11. Finish pinning by overlapping the ends of the facing by ¼ inch. Trim away any excess facing.

12. Baste the facing in position and remove the pins.

13. Machine stitch ⅛ inch inside the raw edge of the facing. Start and end at the underarm seam. Remove the basting.

14. Clip the facing and armhole seam allowances at ½-inch intervals, cutting up to, but not into, the stitching.

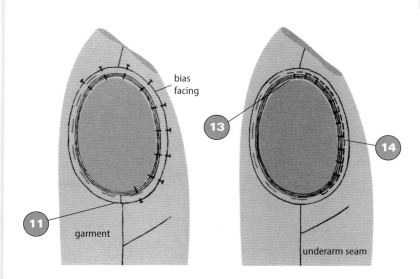

bias facing

garment

underarm seam

Bias-Faced Sleeveless Armholes
Finishing the bias facing

15. Turn the garment wrong side out. Arrange the armhole over the narrow end of the ironing board.

16. Turn the facing to the wrong side of the garment, rolling the facing between your fingers so that the seam is just inside the garment edge. Press, then pin every 4 or 5 inches.

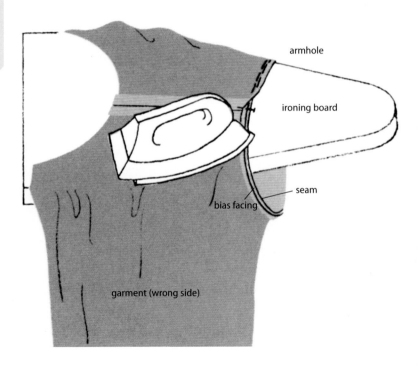

armhole

ironing board

seam

bias facing

garment (wrong side)

17. Slip stitch *(page 145)* the folded edge of the facing to the underlining of the garment. Remove the pins.

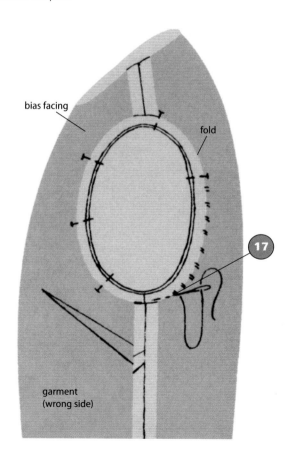

bias facing

fold

garment
(wrong side)

17

Restyling

If you have a shirt you like, but the sleeves aren't quite right, change them! Use these easy approaches to modify sleeves to suit your style.

Changing Long, Full Sleeves Into Short, Flared Sleeves, page 86

Changing Puffed Sleeves into Set-In Sleeves, page 96

Changing Sleeves into Sleeveless Armholes,
page 102

Changing Long, Full Sleeves into Short, Flared Sleeves

Preparing the garment and the pattern

1. To see if your sleeve is wide enough to restyle, measure around its fullest part—usually just above the cuff. Measure the hemline of your flared sleeve pattern. If the pattern hem is over 6 inches longer than the sleeve measurement, you cannot restyle your sleeves by this technique.

2. Carefully remove the sleeves from the garment. Either remove the cuffs or open up the sleeve hems.

RESTYLING

3. Open the underarm seams of both sleeves and remove any ease stitching from the sleeve caps and cuff edges. Press the sleeve fabric flat.

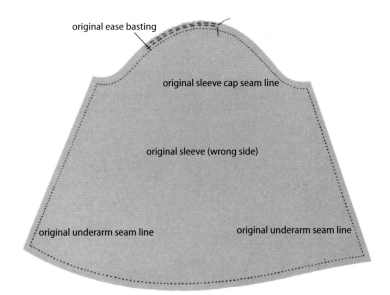

original ease basting

original sleeve cap seam line

original sleeve (wrong side)

original underarm seam line

original underarm seam line

Changing Long, Full Sleeves into Short, Flared Sleeves

Preparing the garment and the pattern

4. If your pattern is for a puffed or gathered sleeve cap, skip to Step 10.

5. If your pattern is for a regular set-in sleeve, which will require 1½ inches of ease in the cap seam, measure the armhole seam line of the garment and the sleeve cap seam line of the pattern. Then subtract the garment measurement from the pattern measurement to determine the amount of ease in the pattern. If the ease is 1½ inches or more, skip to Step 10.

6. If the ease is less than 1½ inches, subtract the figure determined in Step 5 from 1½ inches to find the amount of extra ease you must add to the pattern.

7. To add ease to the sleeve pattern, first draw a line that parallels the grain-line arrow and extends from the pattern dot at the mid-point of the sleeve cap seam line to the hem edge. Then cut the pattern along the line.

8. Tape the pieces of the sleeve pattern to a strip of paper, keeping the cut center edges parallel and separated by the amount of ease to be added (*Step 6*).

9. Draw the sleeve cap seam and cutting lines and the hemline on the strip of paper by extending the original lines. Then mark a new mid-point dot on the sleeve cap seam line midway between the cut edges of the pattern. Trim the excess paper along the cutting lines.

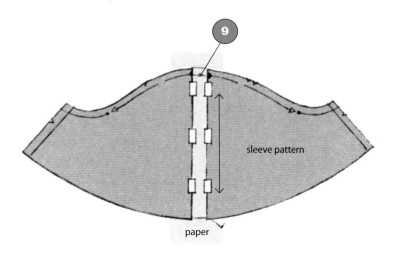

sleeve pattern

paper

10. Place the original sleeves together, wrong sides out.

11. Arrange the sleeve pattern on the fabric so the grain-line arrow is either parallel to the lengthwise grain of the fabric or on the true bias depending on how the pattern fits best. The hem and seam lines of the pattern should not extend beyond the original sleeve seam lines if these have left marks on the fabric.

12. If the pattern fits within the edges of your fabric, pin it in place. Then cut out and mark the sleeves. Skip to Step 21.

13. If you cannot arrange the pattern within the edges of your fabric, the sleeves will need to be pieced with gussets.

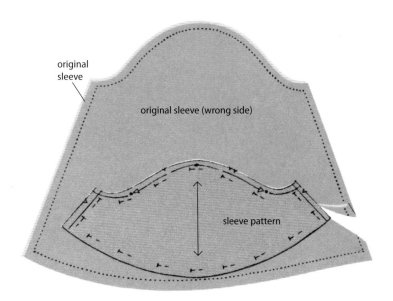

original sleeve

original sleeve (wrong side)

sleeve pattern

Changing Long, Full Sleeves into Short, Flared Sleeves

Piecing the sleeves with gussets

14. If piecing is required, arrange the sleeve pattern on the fabric with the grain-line arrow parallel to the lengthwise grain of the fabric. Center the pattern so the hem edge extends beyond the fabric equally at both underarm seam lines. Insert a few pins at the center of the pattern to hold it in place.

15. At each end of the pattern hemline, mark the point where the hemline intersects the underarm seam line on the fabric. Then make marks along the sleeve cap seam line of the pattern ¾ inch inside the underarm seam lines. Draw new underarm seam lines by connecting each set of marks.

16. Cut the pattern apart along the new underarm seam lines drawn in Step 15.

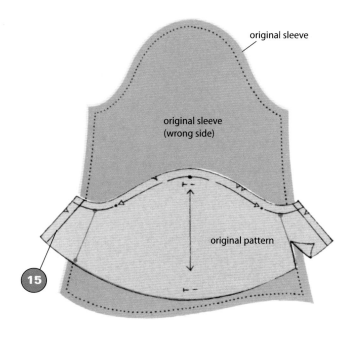

original sleeve

original sleeve
(wrong side)

original pattern

15

17. To make a pattern for the underarm gussets, first fold under the underarm seam allowances of the two small segments of the sleeve pattern cut in Step 16. Then tape the pattern segments together, aligning the original underarm seam lines and matching the sleeve cap seam lines and the hemlines.

18. Pin the gusset pattern to the sleeve fabric. To ensure the best match of the fabric grains along the new underarm seam lines, arrange the gusset so the original underarm seam marking is on the true bias.

19. Pin the main sleeve pattern to the fabric.

20. Cut out and mark the gusset and main sleeve sections. Along the new underarm edges, cut ⅜ inch outside the pattern edges; along the hems and sleeve cap edges, cut along the edges of the pattern. You need not mark the underarm seam lines, but be sure to mark the gussets at the point where the original underarm seam line intersects the sleeve cap seam line.

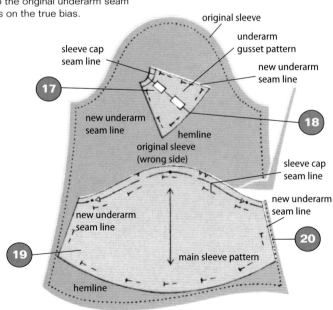

original sleeve

sleeve cap
seam line

underarm
gusset pattern

new underarm
seam line

new underarm
seam line

hemline

original sleeve
(wrong side)

sleeve cap
seam line

new underarm
seam line

new underarm
seam line

main sleeve pattern

hemline

Changing Long, Full Sleeves
into Short, Flared Sleeves
Assembling the sleeves

21. Place a sleeve, or the main section of a sleeve to be pieced with a gusset, wrong side up.

22. Run a line of machine basting—at 6 stitches to the inch—just outside the sleeve cap seam line between the pattern dots indicating the area to be eased. Make a second line of basting ¼ inch outside the first one. Leave several inches of loose thread at both ends of each line.

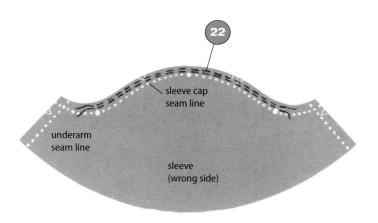

sleeve cap
seam line

underarm
seam line

sleeve
(wrong side)

23a. To assemble a sleeve cut in one piece, fold it in half, wrong sides out. Align and pin along the underarm seam-line markings. Then baste and remove the pins.

24a. Machine stitch and remove the basting. Press open the seam allowances.

25a. Pull up the loose threads of the ease basting on the sleeve cap to shorten the lines of stitches by about 1½ inches, Distribute the gathers evenly.

26a. Repeat Steps 21–25a to assemble the other sleeve.

23b. To assemble a sleeve pieced with a gusset, place the main sleeve section and the gusset together, wrong sides out. Align and pin along the underarm edges, then baste the underarm seams ¼ inch inside the edges and remove the pins.

24b. Machine stitch the underarm seams ⅜ inch from the edges and remove the basting. Press open the seam allowances.

25b. Pull up the loose threads of the ease basting on the sleeve cap to shorten the lines of stitches by about 1½ inches. Distribute the gathers evenly.

26b. Repeat Steps 21–25b to assemble the other sleeve.

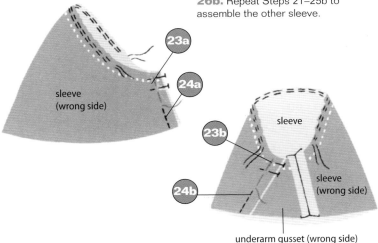

sleeve
(wrong side)

23a

24a

sleeve

23b

sleeve
(wrong side)

24b

underarm gusset (wrong side)

Changing Long, Full Sleeves into Short, Flared Sleeves
Attaching the sleeves

27. Turn the garment wrong side out and turn the sleeves right side out.

28. Slip the sleeve into the armhole of the garment; align the seam-line markings on the sleeve with the original armhole stitching line on the garment. Match the mid-point mark on the sleeve cap seam line with the garment shoulder seam; pin. Match the underarm sleeve seam (the mid-point mark on a pieced-sleeve gusset) with the garment underarm seam; pin.

29. Pin the sleeve to the garment along the part that is not eased.

30. Adjust the ease basting on the sleeve until the sleeve cap fits properly into the armhole and redistribute the gathers evenly. Then pin the sleeve cap to the garment.

31. Baste and remove the pins.

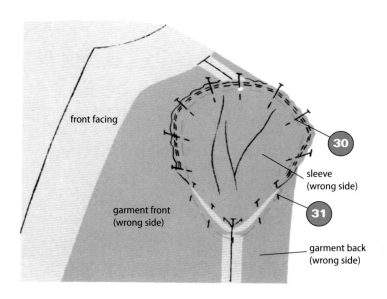

front facing

garment front
(wrong side)

30

sleeve
(wrong side)

31

garment back
(wrong side)

32. Machine stitch the sleeve to the garment, sewing with the sleeve fabric facing up. Remove the basting holding the sleeve to the garment, but do not remove the ease basting.

33. Around the armhole, trim the sleeve seam allowance so it is even with the garment seam allowance.

34. Stitch the seam allowances together around the armhole with a line of machine zigzag stitches or by hand with an overcast stitch (page 144).

35. Press the armhole seam allowances toward the sleeve.

36. Repeat Steps 28–35 to attach the other sleeve.

37. Finish the sleeve hems, following the instructions in your pattern.

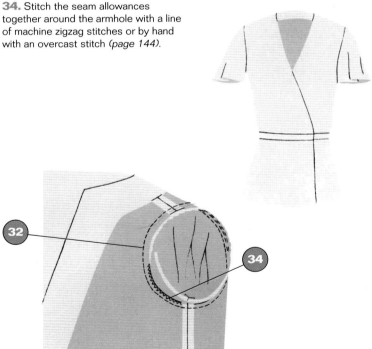

Changing Puffed Sleeves into Set-in Sleeves

Preparing the garment

1. Carefully remove the sleeves from the garment.

Preparing the sleeves

2. On each sleeve, mark the ends of the sleeve cap ease basting by making a line of running stitches perpendicular to the sleeve cap seam line.

3. Remove the ease basting and press the sleeve caps flat. Do not open the underarm seams.

4. To determine the required length for the new sleeve cap seam lines, measure one of the armhole seam lines of the garment and add 1½ inches for ease.

5. To determine how much the original sleeve cap seam lines must be reduced in order to remove the puffs, measure the seam lines and subtract these figures from the new sleeve cap seam lengths *(Step 4)*.

6. If the sleeve cap seam lines must be reduced by more than 1 inch, skip to Step 13.

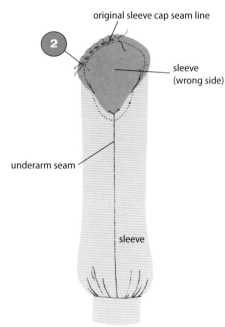

original sleeve cap seam line

2

sleeve
(wrong side)

underarm seam

sleeve

Changing Puffed Sleeves into Set-in Sleeves

Reducing the sleeve cap by 1 inch or less

7. To reduce the sleeve cap seam line by 1 inch or less *(Step 5)*, first turn one sleeve wrong side out and fold it in half lengthwise.

8. Make a chalk mark on the fold at a distance below the original sleeve cap seam line equal to the amount by which the seam line is to be reduced.

9. Starting at the mark made in Step 8, draw a smoothly curved chalk line that gradually tapers to about ½ inch from the original seam line at the running stitches marking the end of the original ease basting. Then run the chalk line smoothly into the original seam line.

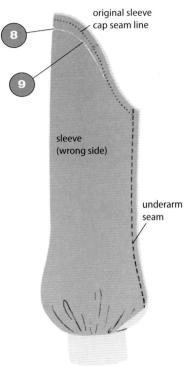

original sleeve
cap seam line

sleeve
(wrong side)

underarm
seam

10. Measure the length of the modified seam line from the underarm seam to the folded center edge. If the measurement is more or less than half the required length determined in Step 4, make a new mark on the folded center edge slightly below or slightly above the mark made in Step 8 and redraw the curve so it measures exactly half the required length.

11. Repeat Steps 8–10 to draw a similarly curved seam line on the other half of the sleeve cap.

12. Mark a new sleeve cap seam line on the other sleeve by repeating Steps 8–11. Skip to Step 19.

Changing Puffed Sleeves into Set-in Sleeves

Reducing the sleeve cap by more than 1 inch

13. To reduce the sleeve cap seam line by more than 1 inch *(Step 5)*, first turn one sleeve wrong side out and fold it in half lengthwise.

14. Make a chalk mark on the fold at a distance below the original sleeve cap seam line equal to 1 inch for the first 1 inch by which the seam line is to be reduced, plus one half of the extra amount over 1 inch.

15. Starting at the mark made in Step 14, draw a smoothly curved chalk line that tapers into the original seam line near the underarm.

16. Measure the length of the new seam line from the underarm seam to the folded center edge. If the measurement is more or less than half the required length determined in Step 4, make a new mark on the folded center edge slightly below or above the original one *(Step 14)* and redraw the curve so it measures exactly half the required length.

17. Repeat Steps 14–16 to draw a similarly curved seam line on the other half of the sleeve cap.

18. Mark a new sleeve cap seam line on the other sleeve by repeating Steps 14–17.

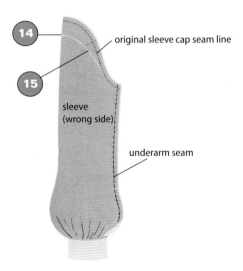

14

15

original sleeve cap seam line

sleeve (wrong side)

underarm seam

Finishing the sleeve

19. Turn the sleeves right side out.

20. On each sleeve, run a line of machine ease basting—at 6 stitches to the inch—just outside the new sleeve cap seam line. Begin and end the stitching midway between the underarm and the running stitch markings made in Step 2. Then make a second line of basting ¼ inch outside the first one. Leave several inches of loose thread at both ends of each line.

21. Pull up the loose thread ends to shorten the ease basting lines on each sleeve by about 1½ inches. Distribute the gathers evenly.

22. Attach the sleeves to the garment, following the instructions for Changing Long Full Sleeves into Short Flared Sleeves (*pages 94–95, Steps 27–36*). However, be sure to try on the garment after the sleeves have been basted in place to be sure the sleeves fit properly.

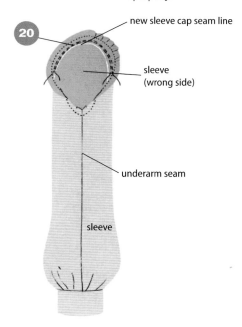

new sleeve cap seam line

sleeve
(wrong side)

underarm seam

sleeve

Changing Sleeves into Sleeveless Armholes

Designing the armholes

1. Carefully remove the sleeves or the armhole facings from the garment.

2a. If you wish to retain the original shape of the armhole, insert pins at 1-inch intervals along the original seam line of one armhole.

3a. Insert pins along the shoulder and the side seams for several inches inside the pinned armhole seam line. Skip to Step 11.

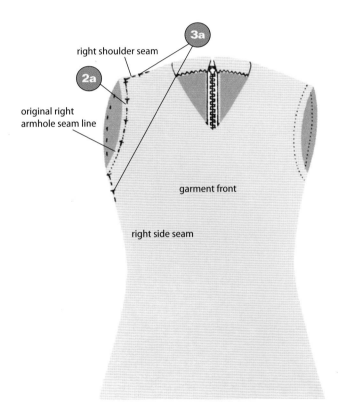

right shoulder seam

3a

2a

original right armhole seam line

garment front

right side seam

Changing Sleeves into Sleeveless Armholes
Designing the armholes

2b. If you wish to create a deeper round or oval armhole, try on the garment and insert a row of pins where you want the new armhole seam line to be. Begin under the arm at the side seam and space pins at 1-inch intervals along the front armhole to the shoulder, then repeat on the back armhole. Be sure not to curve the front armhole seam line so close to the fullest part of the bust that the garment will gap.

3b. Insert pins along the shoulder and the side seams for several inches inside the pinned armhole seam line.

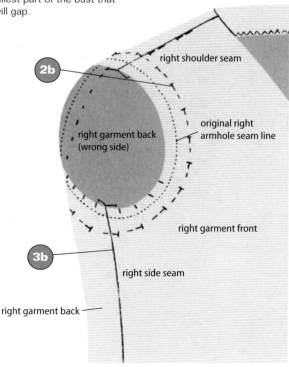

right shoulder seam

2b

right garment back
(wrong side)

original right
armhole seam line

right garment front

3b

right side seam

right garment back

2c. If you wish to create a square armhole, try on the garment and insert a row of pins at 1-inch intervals where you want the new armhole seam line to be. Insert the first pin at the underarm seam. To mark the front underarm, angle the pins upward in a shallow curve. Make sure that the underarm curve does not end so close to the bust that the garment will gap. Then mark the rest of the front armhole by pinning straight up to the shoulder seam. Mark the back armhole with pins in a similar manner.

3c. Insert pins along the shoulder and the side seams for several inches inside the pinned armhole seam line.

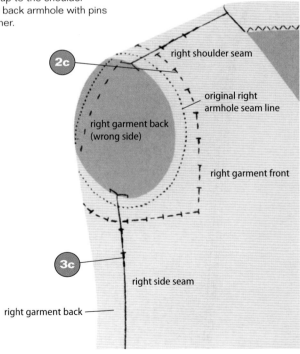

2c

right shoulder seam

original right
armhole seam line

right garment back
(wrong side)

right garment front

3c

right side seam

right garment back

Changing Sleeves into Sleeveless Armholes
Preparing the armholes

4. Run a line of basting stitches along the row of pins marking the new armhole seam line, but do not remove the pins. If the garment is underlined, be sure to baste through both layers of fabric.

5. Draw a cutting line with chalk ⅝ inch outside and parallel to the pinned seam line.

6. Trim away the excess band of fabric from the armhole along the chalk cutting line, but take care to keep the band you cut off in one piece so you can use it as a guide for preparing the other armhole.

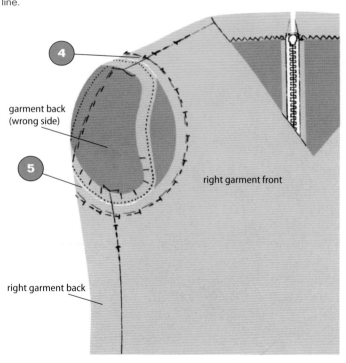

garment back
(wrong side)

right garment front

right garment back

7. Turn the cutoff band of fabric wrong side out and place it over the finished side of the other armhole.

8. Align the fabric band and the garment along the original armhole seam lines and match at the underarm and shoulder seams. Then pin the band to the garment.

9. To mark the new seam line for the armhole, run a line of basting stitches on the garment ⅝ inch inside the fabric band. If the garment is underlined, be sure to baste through both layers of fabric.

10. Trim away the excess fabric from the armhole by cutting along the inner edge of the fabric band.

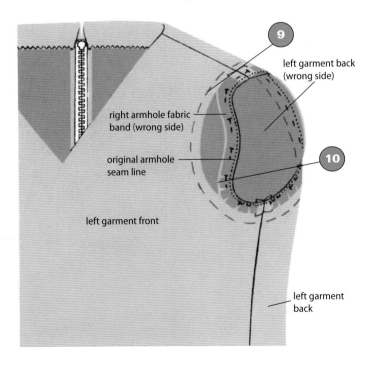

left garment back
(wrong side)

right armhole fabric
band (wrong side)

original armhole
seam line

left garment front

left garment
back

Changing Sleeves into Sleeveless Armholes
Making a muslin pattern for the armhole facings

11. With the garment right side out, slide a piece of cardboard or a magazine into the armhole along which the pins were inserted *(Step 2b or 2c)*. Then place the garment on your work surface with the side and shoulder seams as well as the front armhole facing up. Smooth out the fabric around the armhole.

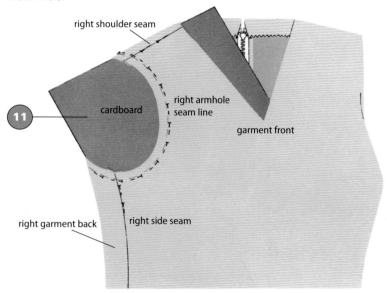

right shoulder seam

right armhole
seam line

11

cardboard

garment front

right garment back

right side seam

12. Cut a piece of muslin, on the lengthwise grain, about 10 inches wide and twice the length of the armhole of the garment between the shoulder and the side seams.

13. Place the muslin over the pinned front armhole, with the lengthwise grain parallel to the lengthwise grain of the garment fabric. Pin the muslin to the fabric.

14. At the underarm, press the muslin with your fingers until you locate the pins inserted along the right side seam. Mark the side seam on the muslin for several inches by rubbing the area with tailor's chalk until the ridges formed by the pins show up as distinct marks on the muslin.

15. Starting at the underarm and working toward the shoulder, press the muslin with your fingers to find the pins marking the new front armhole seam

line. Rub the muslin with the tailor's chalk along the line of pins until the impressions of the pins show up distinctly.

16. Near the shoulder, readjust the folded garment, if necessary, so the shoulder seam faces up, and smooth out the garment fabric and the muslin. Continue to rub the muslin along the pins until you reach the shoulder seam. Then rub for several inches along the pins marking the shoulder seam.

17. Label the muslin rubbing "front." Remove the pins holding the muslin to the garment and remove the muslin.

18. Turn the garment so the right-back armhole faces up and repeat Steps 11–16 to make a rubbing of the back armhole, shoulder and side seam lines. Mark this rubbing "back," unpin it and remove all the pins from the garment.

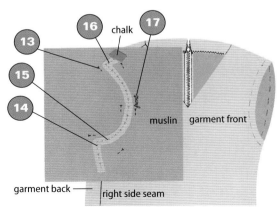

Changing Sleeves into Sleeveless Armholes
Finishing the pattern for the armhole facings

19. Place the muslin pattern for the front armhole facing with the rubbed side up.

20. Remark the rubbed seam lines with pencil, using a straight ruler to even out the shoulder and side seam lines, a curved one to smooth the armhole seam line.

21. Mark cutting lines ⅝ inch outside and parallel to the armhole and side seam lines.

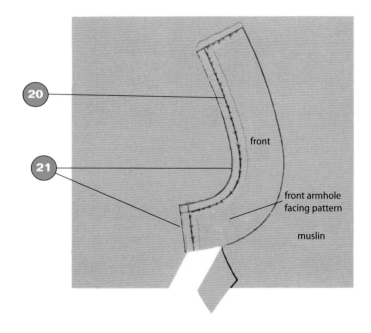

front

front armhole
facing pattern

muslin

22. Mark the inner edge of the front facing pattern by drawing a line from the shoulder seam line to the side cutting line 1½ inches inside and parallel to the armhole seam line.

23. Cut out the muslin pattern along the side and armhole cutting lines, the shoulder seam line and the inner edge.

24. Place the muslin pattern for the back armhole facing with the rubbed side up and repeat Steps 20–23 to complete the pattern.

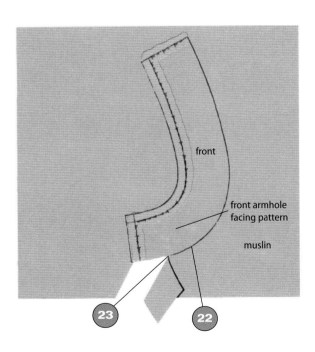

front

front armhole
facing pattern

muslin

Changing Sleeves into Sleeveless Armholes
Finishing the pattern for the armhole facings

25. Place the muslin pattern pieces for the front and the back armhole facings with the marked sides up. Align the patterns at the shoulder edges and tape them together.

26. Draw a grain-line arrow across the shoulder area perpendicular to the taped shoulder line.

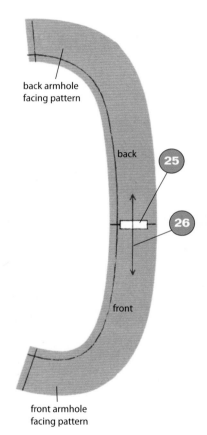

back armhole
facing pattern

back

25

26

front

front armhole
facing pattern

Fitting the armholes

27. Try on the garment. If the armholes gap slightly near the front underarms, insert a pin perpendicular to the seam line at both ends of the area where gapping occurs.

28. Remove the garment and measure the seam line of one armhole between the two pins.

29. Run a line of machine ease basting—at 6 stitches to the inch—just outside the seam line of each armhole between the pins. Leave several inches of loose thread at both ends of each line of basting.

30. Try on the garment and draw up the loose ease basting threads until the front armholes fit smoothly. Distribute the gathers.

31. Remove the garment. Remeasure one armhole along the length of the eased portion of the seam line. Remove the pins.

32. Repeat Steps 27–31 to correct any gapping along the back armholes.

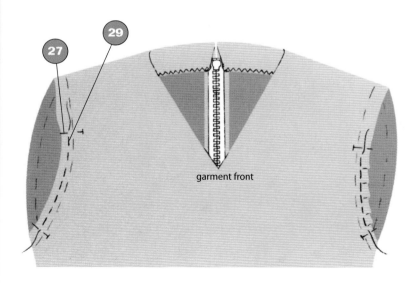

garment front

Changing Sleeves into Sleeveless Armholes
Fitting the armholes

33. Subtract the measurement made in Step 31 from the one made in Step 28 to determine the amount by which you must reduce the length of the armhole seam line on the muslin facing pattern so the facings will fit the eased garment armholes properly.

34. Place the armhole facing pattern marked side up. Fold a tuck, of the width determined in Step 33, along the armhole seam line. Make the tuck in the same general location on the seam line as the easing on the garment armholes, and taper the tuck to a point at the inner edge of the pattern. Pin.

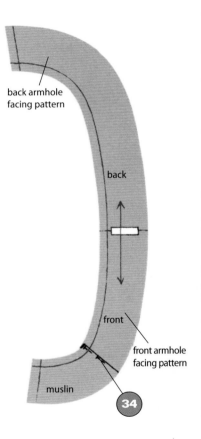

back armhole
facing pattern

back

front

front armhole
facing pattern

muslin

34

Making and attaching the facings

35. Cut a rectangle on the lengthwise grain of your lining fabric, making it slightly longer than the length of the armhole facing pattern and slightly more than twice the pattern width. Then fold the lining in half lengthwise with the wrong sides out.

36. Arrange the armhole facing pattern on the lining with the grain-line arrow parallel to the fold. Pin.

37. Cut out the facings and transfer the pattern markings with a tracing wheel and dressmaker's carbon.

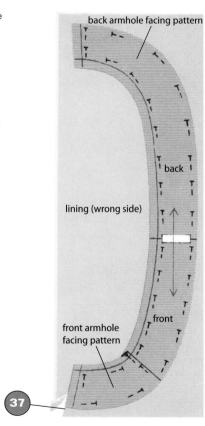

back armhole facing pattern

back

lining (wrong side)

front

front armhole facing pattern

37

Changing Sleeves into Sleeveless Armholes
Making and attaching the facings

38. Pin together each facing, wrong side out, along the underarm seam markings. Then machine stitch the underarm seams of the facings and remove the pins.

39. Press open the underarm seam allowances of the facings.

40. Finish the raw inner edge of each facing with machine zigzag stitching.

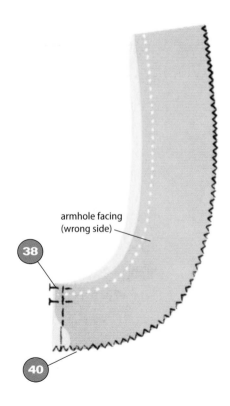

armhole facing
(wrong side)

41. Place the right armhole facing, wrong side out, over the finished side of the right garment armhole. Pin along the armhole seam-line markings, matching the side seams and the shoulders.

42. Machine stitch along the armhole seam-line markings, beginning and ending at the underarm. Remove the pins and the basting along the garment seam line.

43. Trim the armhole seam allowances to ¼ inch.

44. Clip the seam allowances at 1-inch intervals, cutting up to but not into the stitching.

45. Repeat Steps 41–44 to attach the left armhole facing.

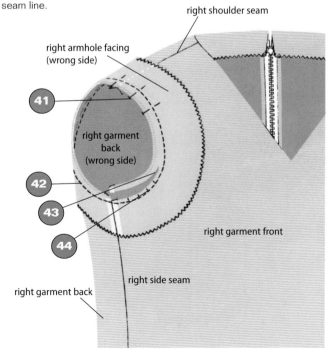

right shoulder seam

right armhole facing
(wrong side)

41

right garment
back
(wrong side)

42

43

44

right garment front

right side seam

right garment back

Changing Sleeves into Sleeveless Armholes
Finishing the armholes

46. Extend the armhole facings and the seam allowances away from the garment and press.

47. To prevent the facings from rolling out and showing on the finished garment, run a line of machine stitching—called understitching—around each facing and through the seam allowances beneath. Stitch as close to the armhole seams as possible.

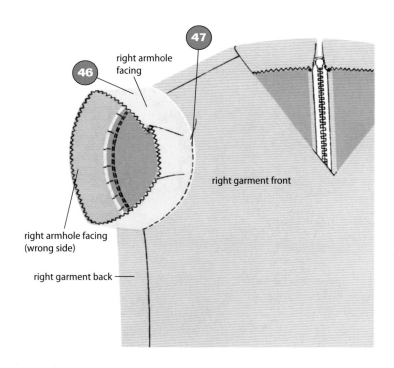

right armhole facing

right garment front

right armhole facing (wrong side)

right garment back

48. Turn the garment wrong side out. Turn the armhole facings to the inside and press.

49. Pin the facings to the garment at the shoulder and the side seams. Attach the facings to the garment seam allowances with hemming stitches (*page 143*). Remove the pins.

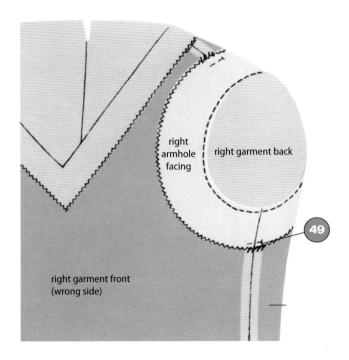

right armhole facing

right garment back

right garment front (wrong side)

49

Appendix

Whether you're trying a new technique or remembering an old one, sometimes you need more details than the pattern instructions offer. Get the details right with these helpful methods for fitting sleeves and adjusting patterns. Plus, refresh your basic skills by reviewing useful stitches and sewing procedures.

Fitting Set-In Sleeves 122

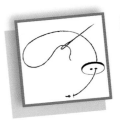

Buttons & Buttonholes . . . 134

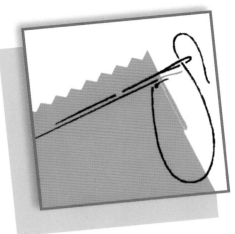

Basic Stitches &
Techniques 140

If the Inset-Sleeve Top is Tight
Symptoms of a tight sleeve top

1. The sleeve top feels snug around the upper arm.

2. Wrinkles radiate from the armhole on both the sleeve top and the shoulder.

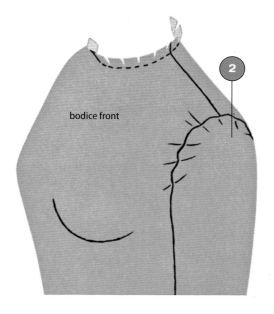

bodice front

Refitting the sleeve top

3. Open the armhole seam around the sleeve top, releasing at least 4 inches on either side of the shoulder seam.

4. Smooth the sleeve top over your upper arm to the armhole at the shoulder seam and fold under enough of the seam allowance of the sleeve top so that it meets the armhole seam line.

5. Pin the folded edge to the armhole seam line of the bodice at the shoulder seam line. Continue folding under the seam allowance from the shoulder seam line around the sleeve, tapering the fold into the original seam line of the sleeve top. Take off the muslin.

6. At the shoulder seam line, measure from the edge of the fold made in Step 4 to the original armhole seam line on the sleeve top.

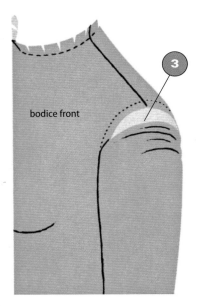

bodice front

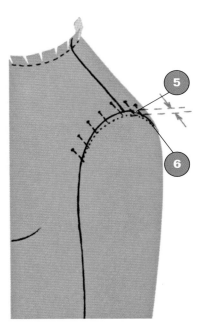

If the Inset-Sleeve Top is Tight
Adjusting the pattern

7. Measure 3 inches down on the sleeve pattern from the center top point of the original seam line, and draw a line at a right angle to the grain-line marking.

8. Cut off the sleeve top along the line made in Step 7.

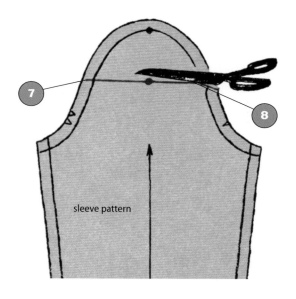

sleeve pattern

9. Slide a piece of shelf paper under the cut pattern and spread until the distance between the edges of the pattern pieces is equal to the measurement made in Step 6. Make sure the edges of the pattern pieces are parallel, then pin them to the shelf paper.

10. On both sides of the sleeve draw new seam lines on the shelf paper joining the original seam lines. Draw new cutting lines ⅝ inch outside the new seam lines and parallel to them. Trim away excess shelf paper.

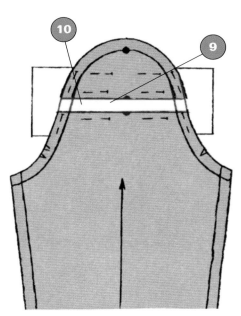

If the Inset-Sleeve Top is Loose

Symptoms of a loose sleeve top

1. The top rolls up above the shoulder seam of the muslin to create a puffed effect.

2. Wrinkles appear across the top along the armhole seam.

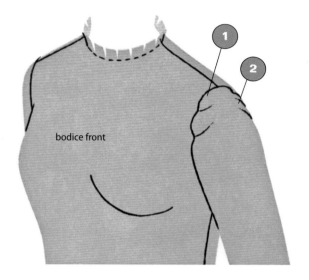

bodice front

Refitting the sleeve top

3. Open the armhole seam around the sleeve top, releasing at least 4 inches of the sleeve top on either side of the shoulder seam.

4. Smooth the sleeve top over your upper arm to the armhole at the shoulder seam, then fold under the fabric at the center edge of the sleeve top. Pin the fold at the point where the shoulder seam line intersects the armhole seam line.

5. Fold under the seam allowance of the sleeve top in front and back and pin it to the armhole seam line, tapering into the original seam line midway down the armhole. Take off the muslin.

6. Turn the muslin wrong side out and measure, at the shoulder seam line, from the new sleeve top seam line to the original one.

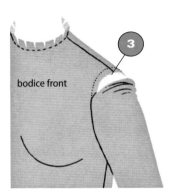

bodice front

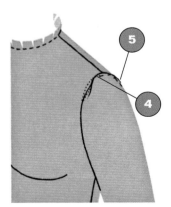

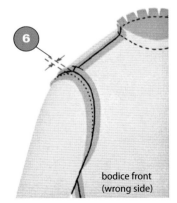

bodice front
(wrong side)

If the Inset-Sleeve Top is Loose
Adjusting the pattern

7. Measure 3 inches down the sleeve pattern from the center top point of the original seam line and draw a line at a right angle to the grain-line marking.

8. Measure from the line made in Step 7 to a point below the line, equal to the distance measured in Step 6; draw a line through the point parallel to the line made in Step 7.

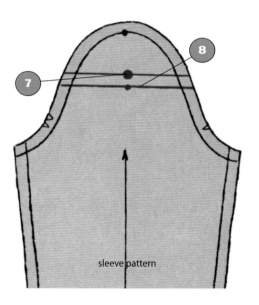

sleeve pattern

9. Fold the pattern so that the two parallel lines meet. Pin this tuck flat.

10. Pin a piece of shelf paper under the tuck.

11. Draw new seam lines on each side of the sleeve from the bottom of the tuck to taper into the original seam line along the top of the sleeve an inch or so above the tuck. Draw new cutting lines on the shelf paper ⅝ inch outside the new seam lines and parallel to them. Trim away the excess shelf paper.

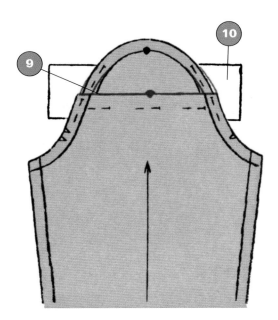

If the Inset-Sleeve Top is Improperly Placed

Symptoms of an improperly placed sleeve top

1. The muslin feels loose in back at the armhole, but tight in front, or vice versa.

2. Wrinkles appear close to the armhole seam line on the loose side of the sleeve top.

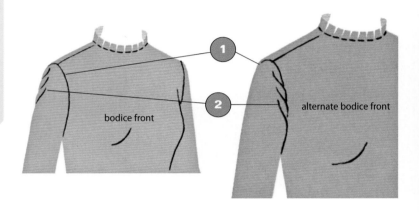

bodice front

alternate bodice front

Refitting the sleeve top

3. Open the armhole seam at the top of the sleeve between the notches on either side of the sleeve top.

4. If the looseness is in the front of the sleeve top, move the center of the sleeve top back from the shoulder seam until the fullness of the sleeve top is evenly distributed. If the looseness is in the back of the sleeve top, move the center of the sleeve top forward.

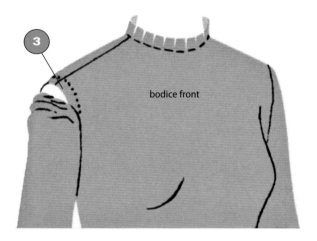

bodice front

If the Inset-Sleeve Top is Improperly Placed
Refitting the sleeve top

5. Pin the seam line of the sleeve top to the armhole seam line of the bodice at the shoulder seam. Take off the muslin.

6. Turn the muslin wrong side out. Measure along the sleeve top seam line from the pin at the shoulder seam to the original pattern mark indicating the shoulder seam attachment point.

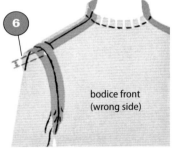

bodice front
(wrong side)

Adjusting the pattern

7. Measure along the sleeve top seam line of the pattern from the original top center marking the distance measured in Step 6 and mark with a dot. Check the notches identifying front and back to be sure that the measurement corresponds in direction to the one made in Step 6.

8. With the ruler at a right angle to the top end of the original grain line, measure the distance measured in Step 6 in the direction used in Step 7 and mark with a dot.

9. Draw a new grain line from this dot to the bottom end of the original grain line.

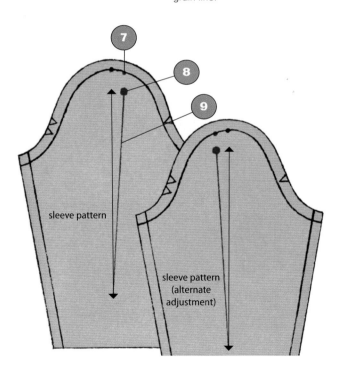

sleeve pattern

sleeve pattern (alternate adjustment)

Measuring the Button

To find the size of your buttonholes, first measure the buttons to be attached. For a flat, thin button, measure its diameter and add ⅛ inch. For a thicker button, measure its diameter and add ¼ inch. For a mounded or ball button, place a thin strip of paper across the mound or ball, pin it tightly in place, slide the paper off, flatten it, then measure it and add ¼ inch.

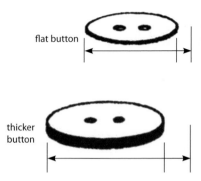

flat button

thicker button

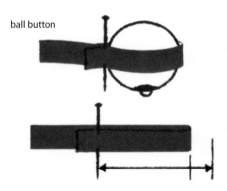

ball button

Buttonhole Stitch

1. Using a knotted thread, insert the needle from the wrong side of the fabric 1/8 inch down from the top edge.

2. Form a loop with the thread by swinging it around in a circle counterclockwise.

3. Insert the needle from the wrong side of the fabric through the same point at which the needle emerged in Step 1, keeping the looped thread under the needle.

4. Draw the thread through, firmly pulling it straight up toward the top edge of the fabric.

5. Repeat Steps 2–4 directly to the left of the first stitch, and continue to make close stitches of even length, forming a firm ridge along the top. End with a fastening stitch *(page 142)* on the wrong side of the fabric.

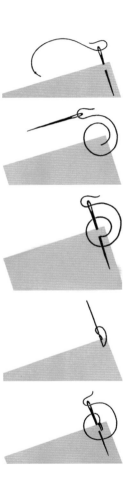

Making Buttonholes

1a. To make a buttonhole entirely by machine, follow the instructions provided with your particular model.

1b. To make a buttonhole without a special accessory, begin halfway between the placement lines and sew tiny machine stitches 1⁄16 inch outside the running stitches that mark the buttonhole position. The stitches should be continuous, pivoting at the corners.

2. With a small pointed scissors, cut the buttonhole along the running stitches, starting in the middle and cutting to each placement line.

3. Sew the buttonhole edges with overcast stitches *(page 144)*, shown in black, to protect them from fraying.

4. Work the overcast edges with a buttonhole stitch *(page 135)*, beginning on the top edge of the buttonhole at the inner placement line.

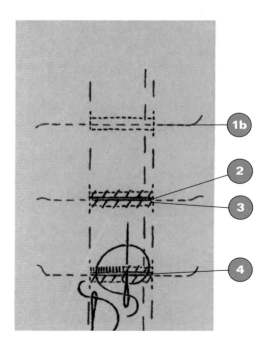

5. At the outer placement line, make five to seven long buttonhole stitches, fanning out about ⅟₁₆ inch beyond the line. Then turn the garment around and repeat for the lower edge. End with a straight vertical stitch at the inner placement line.

6. To finish off the inner edge of the buttonhole with a reinforcement called a bar tack, make three long stitches, side by side, from the top to the bottom edge of the completed rows of buttonhole stitches. These stitches should extend ⅟₁₆ inch beyond the inner placement line.

7. At the bottom edge of the buttonhole, insert the needle horizontally under the three straight stitches made in Step 11, catching the top layer of the fabric underneath. Then pull the needle through, keeping the thread under the needle.

8. Continue to make small stitches across the three long stitches the full depth of the buttonhole.

9. End with two small fastening stitches *(page 142)*.

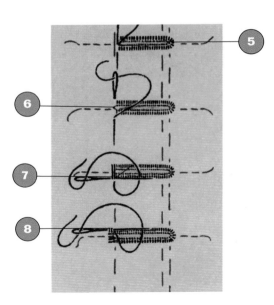

Sewing on Buttons with Holes

1. Using a strand of knotted buttonhole twist, make a small stitch in the fabric at the point where the center of the button is to fall. Insert the needle through one of the holes on the underside of the button and pull the thread through.

2. Hold a wooden kitchen match or a toothpick between the button holes and pull the thread over it as you point the needle down into the other hole. Then make two or three stitches across the match; in the case of a four-hole button, make two rows of parallel stitches across the match.

3. Remove the match and pull the button up, away from the fabric, to the top of the threads.

4. Wind the thread five or six times, tightly, around the loose threads below the button to create a thread shank.

5. End by making a fastening stitch *(page 142)* in the thread shank.

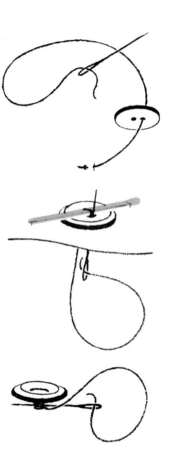

Sewing on Buttons with Shanks

1. Using a strand of knotted buttonhole twist, make a small stitch in the fabric at the point where the center of the button is to fall. Insert the needle through the hole in the shank of the button and pull the thread through.

2. Angle the button away from the fabric with your thumb and take two or three stitches through the button shank.

3. Wind the thread tightly five or six times around the thread shank made in Step 2.

4. End by making a fastening stitch *(page 142)* in the thread shank.

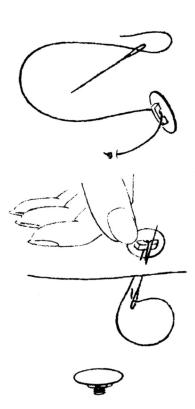

Blind Hemming Stitch

1. Prepare the hem *(pages 150–151)*, then baste the hem to the garment ¼ inch from the edge.

2. Fold the hem along the basting made in Step 1 so that the hem lies underneath the garment and the unstitched edge projects above the garment. Using knotted thread, insert the needle through one or two threads of the garment just below the fold and pull the thread through.

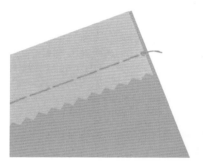

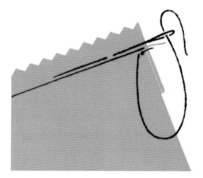

3. Pick up one or two threads just above the fold and ½ inch to the left of the first stitch; pull the thread through. End with a fastening stitch *(page 142)* on the hem fabric.

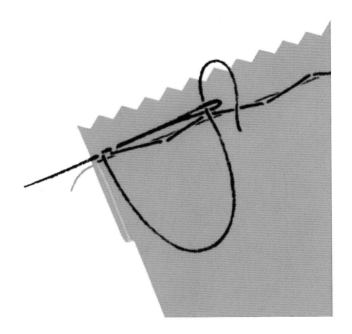

Fastening Stitch

After the last stitch, insert the needle back ¼ inch and bring it out at the point at which the thread last emerged. Make another stitch through these same points for extra firmness. To begin a row with a fastening stitch, leave a 4-inch loose end and make the initial stitch the same way as an ending stitch.

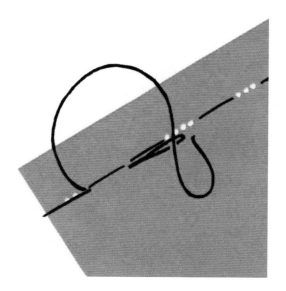

Hemming Stitch

Anchor the first stitch with a knot inside the hem; then pointing the needle up and to the left, pick up one or two threads of the garment fabric close to the hem. Push the needle up through the hem ⅛ inch above the edge; pull the thread through. Continue picking up one or two threads and making ⅛-inch stitches in the hem at intervals of ¼ inch. End with a fastening stitch.

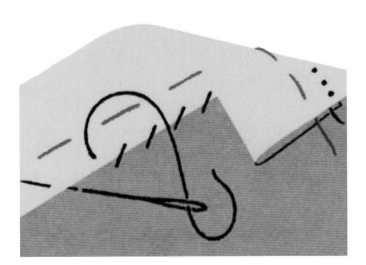

Overcast Stitch

Draw the needle, with knotted thread, through from the wrong side of the fabric ⅛ to ¼ inch down from the top edge. With the thread to the right, insert the needle under the fabric from the wrong side ⅛ to ¼ inch to the left of the first stitch. Continue to make evenly spaced stitches over the fabric edge and end with a fastening stitch.

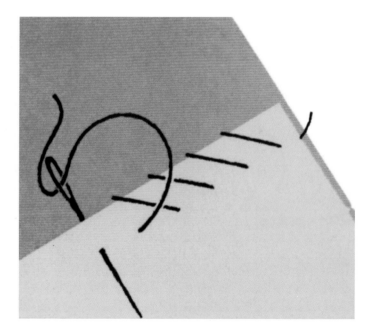

Slip Stitch

Fold under the hem edge and anchor the first stitch with a knot inside the fold. Point the needle to the left. Pick up one or two threads of the garment fabric close to the hem edge, directly below the first stitch, and slide the needle horizontally through the folded edge of the hem ⅛ inch to the left of the previous stitch. End with a fastening stitch.

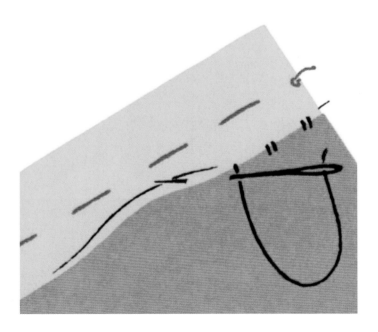

Making and Joining Bias Strips

1. To make bias strips, fold the fabric diagonally, wrong sides together, so that a crosswise edge is aligned with a lengthwise (selvage) edge. Pin the edges together.

2. Cut the fabric along the folded edge. Remove the pins and set aside the top piece of fabric.

3. Determine the number of strips of fabric you will need to make the total length of the strip required; add ½ inch for seam allowances on every strip.

4. To mark off the strips, draw a series of chalk lines parallel to the diagonal edge. Make each strip the desired width, plus 1 inch for seam allowances, if necessary.

5. Trim off both of the selvages,

6. Mark a ¼-inch seam allowance with chalk along the ends of the strips.

7. Cut off the strips along the diagonal chalk lines.

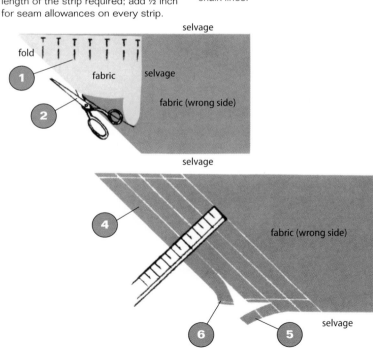

8. Place two strips together, wrong sides out, so that they form a V shape. Align the seam lines and pin.

9. Machine stitch and remove the pins.

10. Repeat Steps 8 and 9 to make one long strip.

11. Press open the seams.

12. Cut both ends of the strip at right angles to the long edges before joining them to another edge.

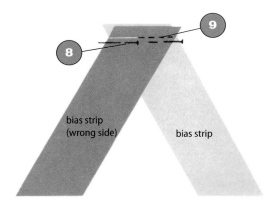

bias strip
(wrong side)

bias strip

Flat-Felled Seams
Preparing to make the flat-felled seam

1. Make a plain seam, with either the right sides—the sides that will be visible in the completed garment—or the wrong sides of the fabric together, depending on your pattern. Press the seam open. Then fold and press both seam allowances in the direction indicated on your pattern.

2. Trim the underneath seam allowance to ⅛ inch.

3. Trim the top seam allowance to ½ inch.

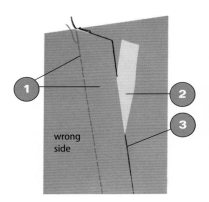

wrong side

Folding the flat-felled seam

4. Fold the top seam allowance over the underneath one, lining up the edge of the top seam allowance along the machine stitching *(blue)* of the original plain seam; this encloses the underneath seam allowance.

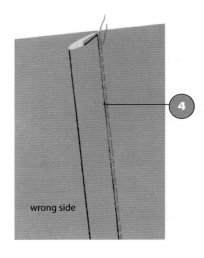

wrong side

Basting and stitching the flat-felled seam

5. Turn the fold to the side on which the felled seam should fall.

6. Pin the felled seam, inserting the pins from the folded edge toward the seam at right angles.

7. Baste (*red*) ⅛ inch from the folded edge.

8. Machine stitch midway between the basting and the folded edge. Remove the basting and press.

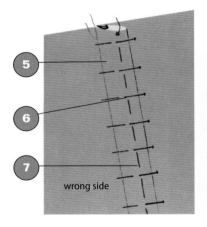

wrong side

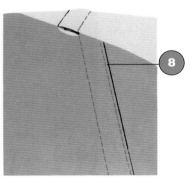

Hong Kong Finish
Preparing to make the hem

1. After marking with pins or chalk the hem length most suitable for your figure, run a line of basting stitches along the markings so that the hemline will be visible on both sides of the garment.

2. With the garment wrong side out, trim the seam allowances of side seams and any other vertical seams to a width of ¼ inch below the basted hemline markings.

3. With a ruler, measure down 2½ inches from the basted hemline marking and make a chalk line all around the edge of the skirt.

4. Trim the raw edge of the hem along the chalk line

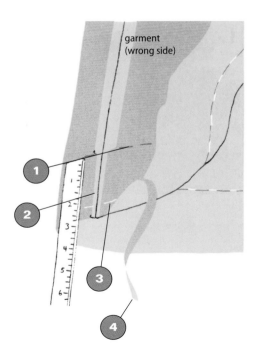

garment (wrong side)

Turning up the hem

5. Turn up the bottom edge of the garment along the basted hemline marking and pin the hem to the garment close to the fold, first matching at the side seams and other vertical seam intersections and then adding more pins between the seam intersections at 1-inch intervals.

6. Pin the raw edge of the hem to the garment, first at the side seams and other vertical seam intersections and then at 6-inch intervals in between, spacing excess fabric fullness evenly between the pins.

7. Try on the garment and adjust the hemline if necessary—basting and pinning it again as described in Steps 1–6.

8. Baste the bottom of the hem to the garment ¼ inch from the folded edge. Remove all pins.

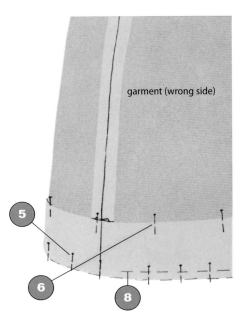

garment (wrong side)

Hong Kong Finish
Preparing the bias strip

9. Measure the circumference of the hem at the raw edge.

10. Cut strips of lining fabric on the bias *(page 146)* 1 inch wide and join the pieces to make a continuous circular strip 1 inch longer than the circumference of the garment at the raw edge. (Alternately, use double-fold bias tape pressed open.)

garment (wrong side)

9

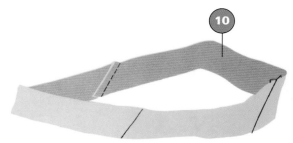

10

Attaching the bias strip

11. With the wrong side of the bias strip facing up, baste and machine stitch the strip to the hem ¼ inch down from the raw edge.

garment (wrong side)

Turning the bias strip

12. Fold the strip over the raw edge of the hem far enough to cover the stitching line made in Step 4. Pin at 1-inch intervals.

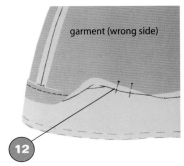

garment (wrong side)

Completing the hem

13. Hand stitch the front of the hem to the folded strip by sewing a line of running stitches directly below the seam line made in Step 4. Remove the pins as you go.

14. Hand stitch the finished hem edge to the garment, with a blind hemming stitch *(page 140).* Remove all bastings and press the hem on the wrong side.

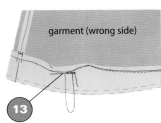

garment (wrong side)

Index

INDEX

Index

Index

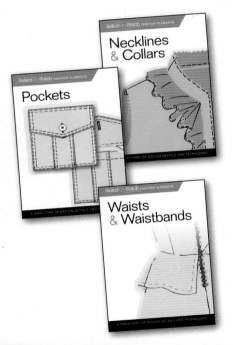